BIRDS FOR
PETS AND PLEASURE

BIRDS

FOR PETS
and PLEASURE

by NEALE HALEY

Illustrated by Pamela Carroll

Delacorte Press / New York

Published by
Delacorte Press
1 Dag Hammarskjold Plaza
New York, N.Y. 10017

"The Basic Aviary: Step-by-Step Directions" by Michael Shays.
Used by permission of the author.

"A Cage or an Aviary for a Cockatiel" by Johonet Wicks.
Used by permission of the author.

Manufactured in the United States of America
First printing

Library of Congress Cataloging in Publication Data

Haley, Neale.
Birds for pets and pleasure.

Bibliography: p.
Includes index.
SUMMARY: Instructions for selecting and purchasing
birds; using cages, aviaries, equipment, and food;
catching, holding, grooming, traveling with,
taming, and training birds; and other aspects
of keeping birds as pets.
1.   Cage-birds—Juvenile literature.
[1.   Birds as pets]   I.   Carroll, Pamela.   II.   Title.
SF461.H23   636.6'862   80-68740
ISBN 0-440-00475-6
ISBN 0-440-00476-4 (lib. bdg.)

To Aunt Beth

My earliest critic—the one who encouraged my childhood attempts as a writer

ACKNOWLEDGMENTS

Birds would never have graced our garden room nor flown through the years in our home if my husband Russ had not shared my interest and made me laugh when things went wrong. This interest has been shared by others who have enriched this book: Michael Shays who wrote the careful instructions on building an aviary, Nancy Shays who shared her knowledge of birds with me, Martha Krueger who answered my endless questions about canaries and parrots, and Johonet Wicks who designed the aviary for cockatiels.

My deepest appreciation goes to Dr. Val Clear, who so meticulously read my manuscript and gave me so many helpful suggestions and comments.

Consultants on smuggling and the importing of birds have included Richard Topper of Lexington, N.C.; Richard Farinato, of Medford, MA; Walter Kilroy of the Division of Law Enforcement for the Massachusetts Society for the Prevention of Cruelty to Animals; and Jim Smith of Bird Land, San Diego, CA.

My appreciation to all those who wrote for *American Cage Bird Magazine*, especially Margie McGee for her informative articles on canaries and Dr. Val Clear whose articles have kept me abreast of import regulations and all phases of aviculture.

I shall always be grateful to Don Murray for his encouragement and editing, to Dr. Arthur Borror for his knowledge and advice on feeding and housing wild birds, and to Jackie Haley for sending out the questionnaires on finches and psittacines.

My special thanks to all the breeders and dealers who answered my questionnaire, especially those marked *
who wrote notes and letters or spoke to me on the phone.

Alabama: Montgomery, Hobby Hunt. *Alaska*: Fairbanks, *Larry Kim of Northern Lights Garden and Pet Center. *Arkansas*: Ft. Smith, Wee Pals Pet Center; Little Rock, Bill's Birds. *California*: Los Angeles, *Jerry Jennings of Walnut Acres Aviaries; *Karoly Gyimesi; Monrovia, *Jim and Barbara McClure of Ranchito Bird Farm; San Diego, *Joe and Pat Aiken; San Marcos, Gene Hall of Fortune Glen Aviaries; Watsonville, *Gilbert Pargeon, Green Valley Bird Ranch; Goleta, *Dougal House. *Connecticut*: Hartford, *Nancy Reed Windsor, Magic Pet Shop. *Florida*: Naples, *Marie Earl Olssen of Trail's End Aviary; *David Delp of Pets and Pisces; Port Walton, *Daphene Earley; Miami, Charles P. Chase Co., Inc.; Sanford, *Michael K. Jackson; Tallahassee, C. Hicks. *Georgia*: Kathleen, Debbie's Aviary. *Illinois*: E. Alton, *Ron and Vickie Betts of Vickie's Aviary; Urbana, *Carol and Paul Peters; Goodfield, *Mel Hunsinger of Glen Aviaries; Chicago, Erling Kjelland, Sedgwick Studio; Palatine, *R. D. Sangster. *Iowa*: Cedar Rapids, Hawkeye Seed Co. *Kansas*: Topeka, Rex's Pet Shop; Wichita, Dick's Animal World. *Kentucky*: Erlanger, *Dale Piatt of Pets-N-Such. *Louisiana*: Shreveport, Bill Sweeters; New Orleans, Wings and Things. *Maine*: Bangor, *Bill Williams, Pets and Passtimes. *Maryland*: College Park, Charles Spalding of House of Hauser's. *Massachusetts*: Cambridge, *Martha Parks of Boston Pet Supply, Inc.; Chicopee, *Hollis Snyder of Pet-O-Rama; Seekonk, *George and Helen Barbary, Barbary Coast Bird World; Somerville, *David Lass of Big Fish, Little Fish. *Michigan*: Grand Rapids, Curious World, Inc. *Minnesota*: Minneapolis, Pat Dragon; Bloomington, *Norman DeLaHunt of Sherwood Pets. *Mississippi*: Jackson, The Fin and Feather; J. D. Pittman of Rebel Feed-Seed Center. *Missouri*: Kansas City, *Mrs. Lyle Bouhardt of Plaza Bird and Pet Supply Co., Inc. *Montana*: Odegaards Evergreen. *Nebraska*: Omaha, *Cheryl Hein of Harry Watts Pet O' Mine Shop; Animal Kingdom. *New Hampshire*: N. Hampton, *L. Rogers Smith of Marroda Pet Shop; Keene, Paul's Pet-Aquarium Center; Hookset, *Evelyn Hastings; Manchester, *Helen Burham. *New Jersey*: Collingswood, *Yvonne Rimi of Unique Pets and Supply Co.; Cimmaminson, *Richard Eckard, Pennsauken. *New York*: Staten Island, *Sandra Beau Sejour; Lindenhurst, R. & G. Feathered Pets; New York, Bronson Tropical Birds. *North Carolina*: Lexington, *Richard Topper, Topper's Bird Ranch. *Ohio*: Middletown, *Bill Kirkpatrick, Exotic Animal Imports; Cincinnati, *Lorraine South of Ewald's Pet Shop; Kent, Sky King's Aviary. *Pennsylvania*: Philadelphia, *For the Birds: Pittsburgh, Pet Pad, Inc. *South Carolina*: John's Island, *B. J. Scott of Terraphanalia Bird Farm. *Texas*: Houston, *Jo Witt; Austin, *Leonard Prado of Prado's Aviary; Munday, *J. C. Baty of Baty's Aviary; Thorndale, *Jo Hall of Shady Grove Aviary; Dallas, Bamboo Pet Shop. *Utah*: Bountiful, Safari Pets. *Virginia*: Richmond, *Len Cohen of Wet N Dri Pets; Chesapeake, Henry Turner; Fairfax, *Judy Hofferman; Falls Church, *Andy Smith; Herndon, *Kevin D. Smith of Smith's Exotic Aviaries. *Washington*: Bellevue, Avi-Cult Pets; Seattle, *June Buckles of Burien Pet and Supply; Robert Mock of Hapsburg Aviary. *West Virginia*: Nitro, *Mr. and Mrs. Charles Davis of Jo-Mars Pet Shop; Morgantown, Lindsay Clark.

CONTENTS

1

HOW TO CHOOSE A BIRD

Few events are more exciting than buying a bird for a pet. Sometimes you know exactly what kind of bird you want. Then you can set about finding the best bird sold in your area—to fit your dream. But if you know nothing about birds, deciding which one to buy will involve looking at as many birds as possible, reading all about them, and asking lots of questions. The choice of birds may be limited, however. Few stores stock a large variety. Most of them sell zebra finches, budgies, cockatiels, canaries, and some parrots.

Finches, darting, colorful, singing birds, find their way into shops everywhere. The most common finch, the zebra finch, is also one of the most active species of birds. Each species can be told apart from all others, and no member of one species can breed and produce fertile offspring with a member of another. Zebra finches come in a multitude of colors from white and gray to buff and chestnut. Bright red bills and legs contrast with the softer color of the feathers. Males and females differ, although both have zebra stripes on the tail in most shades. The male's song sounds a bit like a toy party horn. Zebra finches are perky, alert, talkative, and always into something. A young bird—one that has been out of the nest for nine to twelve days—is easily tamed. It makes a gentle, cuddly pet which will sit in your hand and chirp excitedly when you play with it. Because a finch's bill is small and it won't nip unless you squeeze it, young children like finches as pets.

My friends the Crockers tamed a zebra finch named Coco. They would laugh when Coco zipped across the room to her self-appointed greeting post at the railing's end by the front door. From there she raised a commotion, welcoming everyone in the family who entered. A more amusing, gentle pet would be difficult to find.

Many shops sell other types of finches, but they cost more than zebra finches do. Some of the species which are raised in captivity, and hence are common, include the society (sometimes called Bengalese) finch, silver-bill, and cut-throat finch.

More budgerigars are bred in the United States than any other bird. Most people call budgerigars "parakeets" or "keets." Actually they are just one species of Parakeet, which is a genus, or family. Since there are 115 species of parakeets in the world and many of them are larger than some parrots, to be accurate, you should call your small pet by its right name: budgerigar or budgie.

Budgies act like clowns. They climb, swing, and hang upside down by their feet. The more attention they get, the more they jabber, ring their bells, and show off. They mimic sounds around the house, birds they hear outside, and add a chattering vocabulary of their own which only they understand.

If you buy a young budgie—one less than four months

A tame bird tilts its head to a "preening" finger on the back of its neck.

old—you will be able to train it to sit on your finger. In time you may even teach it to mimic simple words. Budgies also learn to talk in simple phrases. Certain sounds such as "pretty bird" seem to please them. Male budgies usually learn to mimic more words than females. However, contrary to what most people say, females may tame more easily and become more loving and gentle pets. Until they are tame, however, they bite harder than males. All budgies are alike under their feathers, although the colors vary from the original green to rainbow hues of yellow, soft blue, and violet. Budgies are hook-bills, the name given to a group of birds whose bills hook over on the tip and have a sharp cutting edge for breaking nuts and seeds. Though a budgie may grip your finger, it won't hurt unless you yank your hand away and rip it on the edge of the bill.

Unfortunately budgies are a bit prone to sicknesses not found in other birds. Some are born with a feather condition that prevents them from flying. Others grow deformed bills. Budgies may become nasty if they are neglected.

A gentle person makes the best kind of owner for a cockatiel. The birds themselves have a gentle, almost retiring nature. They are so peaceable, they get along with the smallest finches—a rare quality in the world of nature. A cockatiel needs to learn to trust humans at a young age, even before it is out of the nest. Breeders earn this trust by hand-feeding baby birds, which they then sell directly to individuals. Other birds, sold to stores, tend to be older birds. It takes far more patience and time to train them, but it is not impossible. Cockatiels make one of the best tame birds a child could own.

Cockies are good-natured, interesting, and clean birds. Like all hook-bills they perform stunts in their cages and like to show off. Unlike the parrots, which are their competitors in size and price, cockies entertain themselves rather well when left alone, although they thrive on company. Their sturdy bodies make them easier to handle and more resistant to sickness than smaller birds. A cockie's looks give it distinction. The basic gray plumage makes a soft background color for splashes of white on the wings, and cheeks bright with yellow and orange. A striking crest rises high on its head.

Even untamed cockatiels make unusual pets. I once owned one named Scratch-it who could whistle a haunting melody. Nothing pleased him more than having his head scratched. He would thrust it through the wide openings between his cage bars whenever I entered the room. If I ignored him, he would scold until I came and rubbed his head with my fingernail.

The more expensive cockatiels, such as the albino and pearled, are in such demand that many are overbred and thus weakened. A normal gray cockie is a wiser buy. Every bird has some disadvantages. Cockatiels not only have larger bodies than finches and budgies, but larger membranes for producing sound, so they make a lot more noise than smaller birds. They are also less active. Their retiring nature may make some cockatiels shy or even nervous with too many people around or in a noisy house.

Perhaps the song of a bird brings music to your heart. No bird sings as varied and beautiful a song as the male canary. Now canaries are bred in beautiful colors as well. They may be pinkish, orange, or other colors. Some even flaunt topknots as if wearing floppy hats. My daughter used to wake joyously in the morning when Nary, her canary, acted in place of her alarm clock. Nary sang like liquid sunshine as soon as daylight wove patterns across the quilt on his mistress's bed. Since only males sing varied, long songs, if you buy a canary for its song, be sure to pick a guaranteed male.

Not long ago the U.S. Government lifted a fifty year ban on the importation of parrots. Immediately parrots accounted for over eighty percent of the birds imported. Although parrots have the potential to be marvelous pets, they have such complex characters, it takes great skill and experience to train them. The majority of bird shop owners and parrot breeders I queried in this country felt that children—certainly those under twelve—should not own parrots. A parrot can bite off a child's finger carelessly in play. Only a parrot that is already finger-tamed should be considered as a pet. Breeders in this country take young parrots from the nest at about two weeks of age and hand-feed them so they look upon humans as their parents. Such birds are safe with older children who are gentle in spirit, quiet in manner, and have had some experience handling a smaller psittacine. However there are few domestic breeders and the taming and feeding process takes months, so such birds are not only difficult to find but are expensive as well. It is important the parrot you buy is a young and gentle bird. You should be able to handle it in the pet shop or at the breeder's farm. If the person who sells it is reluctant to let it sit on your hand, it is probably not suitable for a child's pet.

Parrots adapt slowly to change. Many never accept a new owner or a new home. All parrots need a great deal of attention and company. They can make very loud noises. Unhappy parrots screech. Avoid old birds and ones that are sold at low prices. If only it were possible for the amateur to retrain a parrot! But it's not.

In a questionnaire sent to over two hundred shop owners and breeders in every state I asked, "Which bird makes the best first pet?" Four birds topped the list of answers: zebra finches, budgerigars, cockatiels, and canaries. It just happens these are the four most common pet birds in this country.

There are many reasons why they make excellent pets. They are seedeaters. The seed they need is easily available, so you can always feed your pet the correct diet. It is easy to find information on the care of these four species, so they are more likely to survive. They are all raised in captivity, so adjust readily to being confined as pets. When you buy one, you are not caging a bird that has always known freedom. In owning a captivity-raised bird, you are not depleting the wildlife of the world as you would by choosing a less common bird.

There are some other birds that make just as fine pets as the ones listed above. The society finch, for example, is a close second to the zebra finch. Some people prefer it to the zebra finch. The society is an artificial species produced four hundred years ago by the Chinese or Japanese. Since it never existed in the wild, it accepts a cage as its natural habitat. The brown and white color of this bird combines in patterns which make each society finch distinct. It likes people, tames easily when young, and breeds easily. Societies are slightly less active than zebra finches, but are more sociable. In some states, especially in the Northeast, they are rather expensive and difficult to find. Elsewhere they may cost as little as zebra finches do. The finches that are at least as large as zebra finches, such as nuns and the green singing finch, also make good pets. The exception is the Gouldian finch, which, though beautiful, is delicate in the hands of an amateur.

What if you are looking for your *second* bird? You might want to breed birds, for example, either for fun or for a science project at school. Then you do need two. The easiest species to breed are society and zebra finches. Be sure to buy adults that are properly sexed—which means, one male, one female—and that are not brother and sister, since inbreeding may produce deformed off-spring. Someone who raises these species is most likely to sell a breeding pair. Female society finches, however, are so difficult to sex, even the experts may make mistakes.

If you want two birds for company or to watch how they interact with each other, among the trouble-free pairs are the gentle, cooing diamond doves, and the bungling, floor-pacing button quails. Two finches of the *same sex*, if they are friendly, may be kept safely together.

A group of finches, if compatible, may live happily together in an aviary—a large cage or room. Common finches that will not fight with one another include: zebra, society, green singing, and strawberry finches; red-eared, orange-cheeked, and other waxbills; cordon-bleus, and nuns. Avoid cut-throat finches and weavers. An aviary may also be filled with different colored budgies or small-size hook-bills. It is unwise to mix budgies with other species, because they can be mean even to larger birds.

One species, the lovebird, should never be kept in pairs in the same cage (except for breeding), even though lovebirds are commonly sold this way. The cock, the male, will overfeed its mate. Don't be fooled by the love-birds' name: they love each other, not people. They seldom make gentle or tame pets, but will be active, humorous, and colorful to watch. Unfortunately they have a tendency to become nasty and scrappy.

Soft-billed birds, those that eat fruit and nectar rather than seed, should be bought only by the experienced bird-owner. Their diet is complex and must be replen-ished several times a day. Soft food means soft bowels and these cause a messy cage. Small soft-billed birds are delicate. Even if they appear healthy when you buy them, they may live only a few months, because it is so difficult to acclimate them.

Many excellent books describe birds you might find for sale. Among the best authors: Bates and Busenbark who have books on both finches and parrots; Clear, *Common Cagebirds In America*; and Rogers, *Encyclopedia of Cage and Aviary Birds*.

Almost any bird makes a good pet if you know about its nature and understand its needs. Whichever bird you choose will become part of the family as much as a cat or dog would. It may fly to greet you as Coco flew to the front door when her family came home, or it may sing "like liquid sunshine" as Nary sang, or it may scold until you scratch its head as Scratch-it the cockatiel did. Think, read, compare; then listen to your heart when you buy a bird.

2

TIPS ON BUYING
A BIRD

One bird will live happily and safely in a cage. As soon as you place two together, problems may arise. A child with a first pet usually fails to recognize trouble, and one bird or the other suffers. A pair of adult male and female finches may peck each other lovingly until one is bald on the neck. At least once a year birds molt, which means losing old feathers and growing new ones. Molting takes energy, so a bird may feel listless and want to be alone. Its mate, however, may still have lots of energy and pester it or even injure it. You can separate birds in molt, if you notice in time, but it takes experience to recognize the symptoms. Also, females sometimes feel weak for a day when laying an egg, and most of them lay eggs whether they have nests or not. The male may try to make her fly.

Hook-bills, though they preen each other, are not as likely to peck each other bald. However, in their courtship ritual, the cock feeds the hen, the female. Even if they are not breeding, the cock may feed the hen by coughing up the food he eats. Unless the owner realizes the cock is growing thin, the bird may starve, while the hen could become sick from growing too fat. Two birds sometimes fight. Budgies of the same sex do. So a wise buyer starts with one bird. When he has some experience and does buy two, he either chooses finches of the same sex, keeps them in separate cages, or houses them in an aviary large enough to prevent boredom and pestering.

The best place to buy a bird is from a breeder near your home. Breeders tend to have healthy birds. They have to know a lot about birds to breed them, and they will pass this knowledge on to you. Many small breeders don't advertise. You may discover who these breeders are by asking people who own birds, especially those with several birds. Bird clubs and breeders are also listed in bird magazines such as the *American Cage Bird Magazine, Bird World: American Aviculturists' Gazette,* and *The AFA Watchbird.* They are your best source for cockatiels and parrots. Large breeders may place advertisements in your local newspaper and telephone book.

Many pet stores sell birds that are bred locally. All you have to do is ask where their birds come from. Almost all canaries and a large portion of budgies and zebra finches found in stores are raised in this country. When you long for a rarer species as a second bird, the bird magazines list domestic breeders who ship birds by air.

State regulations often make it easier for pet stores to sell imported rather than domestic birds. Imported birds are either cage-bred in a foreign country or captured in the wild. Zebra finches, budgies, and cockatiels are *all* cage-bred because Australia, their native land, bans the export of its birds. The unusual species, especially parrots, are generally caught in the wild. For every wild bird that reaches a store alive, a great many have died on the way. Many also die during their first year in captivity as a result of changes in diet and because of mishandling.

Here are some clues to help you tell whether a pet store or a breeding farm sells healthy birds. Look around carefully and don't be afraid to ask questions. The bird area should look clean and smell sweet. The cages should have fresh paper on the floors. The perches and the sides and bottoms of the cages should not be caked with droppings. Note if the drinking water looks clear and sparkling and if the seed containers are full and free of dirt, droppings, and chaff. The manager should be able to answer questions about the birds' diets, where they come from, and how to care for them. A small clue to his knowledge of birds shows in the seeds he feeds: it should come in large bags, not in small boxes, although he may also sell small boxes of seed.

Finally examine the birds themselves. Healthy birds hop and fly about and their eyes shine. The feathers look sleek and neat. Every few minutes the birds snap up some seeds to eat. When someone tries to catch them, they evade the net over and over again.

Birds with puffy feathers sticking out at angles or who sleep on the floor of the cage are molting heavily or are sick. Don't buy a bird in molt, or a sick one either, because you feel sorry for it. Most sick birds die. Ruffled, dull feathers and bare spots point to poor care. Birds in crowded cages easily develop illnesses. Once in a pet store in Maine I saw six cockatiels in a cage built for one budgie. They couldn't climb or fly without jostling one another. A store in Florida kept each cockatiel in a spacious, separate cage. You can guess which birds were healthier. If *any* bird in a place looks sick, don't buy a bird there.

An injured bird may be on sale for a low price, but

An aviary is a promise of freedom, longer life, and exercise for flight muscles—the best gift you can give your bird.

think how you will feel apologizing for it later if you buy it. Once, when a friend noticed the missing toenail on one of my diamond doves, I explained it had been that way when I bought the bird. But I wondered if my friend thought *I* had neglected it.

It is a good idea to check the differences between several stores in your area before you buy a bird. Once you decide on the species you want, choose the healthiest bird available, regardless of price. Cheap birds may have been culled from a breeder's flocks because they were weak or old. Bargain prices may mean the bird was smuggled into the country. States close to the Mexican border, which smugglers cross over easily, and in Florida, where smuggled birds arrive by boat, are frequent trouble spots; but illegal birds crop up in almost any state. Smuggled birds have never been checked for sickness and could be carriers of bird diseases.

If you are buying a bird to tame, learn from books or by asking questions how to recognize an immature bird —one decked in its baby plumage—since only immature birds can be tamed. For example, immature zebra finches (except white ones) have black bills. When the bills turn half orange, the finches are too old to tame. Very young gray males have tiny black tips on a few breast feathers. Immature budgies—called barheads—have black, wavy lines ridging their foreheads. When the ridges disappear, the budgie is much more difficult to tame. Immature cockatiels have pale face markings, or the orange and yellow markings on the face are just starting to show. Their bills and feet have a pinkish tinge. Normal male cockatiels have adult colors you can recognize by the time they are nine months old. But they are only tamed easily when they are less than four months old.

A canary, on the other hand, ought to have reached

adulthood before being sold. Most buyers want a singing canary, which means a male. Even experts have trouble telling the sex of canaries before they are eight months old. You may be able to pick a singing canary yourself by *watching* and listening to it sing. Its throat should swell out and look full and rounded. A female canary may sing, too, but the song has fewer notes and variations than a male's and ends with a *jerk of the head*. It pays to spend a long time watching and listening in the store.

If you intend to breed birds, you need a guaranteed pair. In many species the coloring of the adult bird signifies its sex. In all colors of zebra finches except white, the male has orange cheek patches. Sexing is more difficult with white ones. The male will sing and his bill is usually redder than the female's. An adult budgie has a different color cere, which is the fleshy piece above the bill that has the nostril holes in it. It is blue in males; brown in females. However, sometimes the cere appears neither blue nor brown, because the bird may lose the blue or brown color when it is not ready to nest.

When you have finally chosen your bird, be ready to take it home safely. Pet stores will put the bird in a box, but the box is usually flimsy. It collapses easily and has no insulation against changes in temperature. Take a corrugated cardboard box with you, so the bird will be safer on the trip. The box should be small enough to fit under your jacket. Punch many holes in it for ventilation and cut a door in one side that can be taped shut behind the bird. Or you may place the carrying box the store supplies into a well-ventilated cardboard carton.

Once your bird is boxed to take home, wait a moment to feel the temperature in the store. Often it runs around eighty degrees F (twenty-seven degrees C). Since your bird needs to stay warm to arrive home safely, tuck the box under your coat. Be sure air circulates around the box so the bird won't suffocate. Once, at Christmas, I watched two girls in New Hampshire carry a boxed bird along the street. Down jackets protected the girls, but no one warned them to protect their bird. Even in warm weather the change in temperature may cause problems. The store may be warmer than your air-conditioned house. Birds adjust to temperature changes that increase or decrease about ten degrees in an hour. Quicker changes shock a bird's system. You may need to keep your bird in a warm room or place a lamp by its cage for an hour or two when it arrives home until it adjusts to the new temperature.

If you are traveling by car, never leave a bird in a box inside the trunk. Automobile trunks have no protection from exhaust fumes, which can kill a bird. Leaving a bird in the car in the sun will kill it.

The bird in the box you carry has changed owners without knowing it. Until you bought it, it shared the world with other birds. Now it depends on you not just for food, but for companionship as well. As a pet, it needs you.

3

A BIRD NEEDS MORE THAN FOOD

When you bring a bird home, it needs time by itself to adjust to its new surroundings. Then it settles down. It finds its food dishes and learns how to land on the perches or climb up the sides of its cage. It usually takes two or three days for a bird to adjust to a new location.

Finches and canaries flutter against the cage bars and can injure themselves when they are frightened. They often panic in new quarters, especially with strangers close by. Once a bird calms down, you will be able to approach it without terrifying it. Always walk slowly without any jerky movements. Birds that are wild by nature or have never been close to people may continue to flutter at the sight of you for many days or weeks. It helps to speak softly and sweetly or whistle to a bird. It listens to the sound and in time will associate the sound with a friend.

Parrots have the most difficult time of all birds in accepting change. They are ultraconservatives by nature. When you bring an untamed parrot home, keep it iso-

lated for three or four days. Cover a portion of the cage
to give it a place to retreat. Be sure it has plenty of food
and water—but no visitors. It needs this time to settle
down. A new parrot in one house was so nervous and
upset, it plucked out all its feathers. A quiet location is
important for cockatiels, too, although they are less sensi-
tive than parrots.

A finger-tamed bird, on the other hand, must not be
isolated. It needs constant loving attention both for comfort in its new surroundings, and in order to stay tame
and responsive. Every day it should have the joy of
being handled.

Some birds, especially hook-bills, dislike change so
much, they feel too upset to eat the first few days in a
new place. Lime Sherbert, a budgie lent to me, ate so
little it worried me. I tried to think of a treat that might
tempt her to eat her regular seed. A spray of millet—
with the seeds still on the stalk—did the trick. Once she
had sampled the treat, she turned to her seed and made
up for starving herself for three days. Other treats such
as lettuce, a tree limb, or a branch off a forsythia or
honeysuckle bush may tempt your bird to eat. Some birds
are slow to find their seed dishes, so always scatter seed
on the cage floor where they can find it easily the first
few days.

Once a bird adjusts to its surroundings, you may spend
as much time with it as you like. Approach a bird
quietly with slow, even movements. Work patiently with
a new bird, giving it plenty of time to come to know
you. When you put your hand in a parrot's cage, make
a fist—it has no reason to find a fist threatening—and
then it cannot bite you easily. Let a parrot or cockatiel
come to you to make friends rather than forcing yourself

on the bird. They are such intelligent birds, they will grow partially tame even if they were not hand-fed in the nest, provided you are willing to earn their friendship over a period of weeks or months rather than days and you remain loving and gentle at all times.

Parrots have two habits that can cause trouble: they cry out loudly and they chew everything in sight. When a parrot cries or crows, cover the cage with a towel, making it dark inside. Soon whenever it sees the towel coming and knows you are going to quiet it, it will become still. One parrot I know remains quiet while someone is napping if only a small kitchen towel is resting on top of the cage. Of course, you use a towel only for a short time during the training period.

As soon as a parrot arrives, give it a tree branch as thick as your wrist. It will chew it to pieces with pleasure and soon need another one. Wood and plastic toys satisfy a parrot's desire to chew and also keep its bill shortened so it needs less trimming.

All birds need exercise. Finches, canaries, budgies, and cockatiels enjoy flying. Because their muscles are developed for flight, they are healthier if they have a chance to use their wings every day. Check a room first to be sure it is safe. Open windows, electric fans, heaters, stoves, curtains where birds may catch their toenails, poisonous plants, are potential killers. Birds are so curious they climb into anything they can find: pockets, openings behind hangings or pictures, and places humans just can't imagine until a bird goes there. Cover windows with curtains when a bird is loosed the first few times so it won't break its neck dashing against the exposed glass. Someone should be around to watch a bird when it flies free so it does not get into trouble. One woman couldn't find her canary for over twenty-four hours. Then it told her where to look by singing from inside a kitchen drawer.

A tamed bird with its wings clipped cannot exercise by flying. It enjoys the time it spends with you, clambering on your finger and clothes. One budgie I knew never used its cage at all. It spent its time on a tea table playing on swings, seesaws, and toys his mistress kept there for him.

A tame bird will return to its cage on your finger. Other birds may need help finding their way home to their cages. It helps if you fasten a perch so it extends beyond the cage door or hang a porch designed for cages outside the door. Some birds enjoy their freedom so much they refuse to return when you wish. Try placing fresh water and seed, a bath, or a favorite treat inside the cage to lure a bird inside again.

A parrot that is reasonably tame and has its wings clipped may be allowed to climb on top of its cage and sit on a perch mounted there. The cage should be high enough off the floor to prevent the parrot from stepping down and walking away. Although parrots with clipped wings no longer fly, they, too, need exercise by walking or climbing. They find captivity harder to bear than smaller, less intelligent birds. A bored or unhappy bird will pluck out its feathers.

In the wild, birds often congregate in flocks and nest in colonies with many pairs of birds in the same tree. When a bird lives in a cage, it no longer has other birds to fly with or a territory it considers its own and must protect. It needs a substitute for these activities. Making friends with people and flying free may take their place.

4

A HOUSE FOR YOUR BIRD: A CAGE OR AN AVIARY?

A whole assortment of cages hangs on display where birds are sold. Some have bright-colored paints or unusual shapes. But which cage makes the best house for a bird? The choice depends on the amount of freedom the bird will have in its new house, on the cost of the cage, and on whether the bird flies or climbs most of the time.

A tame bird lives with the family, riding about on shoulders or strutting on the floor, so it has hours of freedom. However, a bird that will spend most of its life in a cage will be healthier in the largest cage you can afford or in an aviary. Space—that's the all-important dimension.

A bird's muscles and wings were designed for flight; a bird needs to fly to keep fit. For centuries the small cages used for birds denied them room to exercise. Some books and pet shops describe a "minimum size" cage needed for each species of bird. This is the same as saying *you* belong in a small room where you can exercise only by jumping up and down. You *could* live in such a tiny space, but wouldn't you be happier and healthier with more room?

If you can afford only a small cage, freedom for the bird to fly outside the cage every day will compensate for the confinement. But there is an alternative to a minimum-size cage: an inexpensive homemade aviary. In even a small aviary a bird may fly, swing, build a nest to sleep in, and feel as much at home as a bird in nature's world outdoors. This is true for the climbing psittacines, which are hook-bills, as well as for the flying finches and canaries. A home-built aviary can cost less than a store-bought cage.

Even if you build an aviary for your bird, you will still need a cage for transporting it and keeping it in emergencies. Such a cage need only be the minimum size for the species. The best ones are rectangular in shape and free of trim. If you want curves for the sake of beauty, choose a cage with an arched roof.

All other cages have disadvantages. A round cage must have round papers for the bottom, which take much more time to cut than the square ones, and the curving bars make it difficult to fasten automatic feeders securely. A cage with bars that slant inward allows water to drip out of automatic feeders until they are empty. If the bars slant outward, making the cage wider at the top than at the bottom, the chaff sifts down to the floor whenever a bird breaks seed high in the cage. Overhanging roofs block the placement of feeders high in the cage, which is the best place for water. Extra trim and ornaments collect dirt. Cages sold for breeders will have the simple, plain shape that demands the least time and care.

A cage should be bright metal—chrome, stainless steel, or electroplate. These metals never rust. Painted cages peel or rust in time. Many-storied bamboo cages with their flavor of the exotic East would make delightful places for a budgie to climb, but at the same time the bird would chew its fragile house to bits. Because bamboo is porous, the droppings from the birds never wash off completely.

New cages have rectangular pieces of plastic around the lower fourth of the cage to prevent seed husks from falling out of the cage. If you tape clear plastic wrap about halfway up the side of the cage, less chaff drops on the floor. Never cover the entire cage, because the bird would suffocate.

It's amazing how many people save old bird cages in their attics. When a friend offers to give you an old cage, beware. I have one in my garage with bent wires and holes where seed cups once fit. Only a fat button quail could not escape from it. Old cages often have paint that must be scraped off completely. They should be repainted with nontoxic, unleaded paint because other paints poison birds. The trays in old cages tend to stick, too, which makes it a chore to change the paper. But worst of all the cage might be the wrong size for your bird. Manufacturers make standard-size cages for budgies, canaries, and finches, but remember, "standard size" means the minimum size for your pet.

Each type of bird has special needs. Consider the size of the bird's body. A small bird needs bars that are close together so it does not escape. A finch should have a cage with bars set close together. When my husband and I bought our first birds, four orange-cheeked waxbills, I chose a cylindrical cage because I thought it would look pretty in our garden room. The finches had to learn to fly like helicopters—straight up and down. Finches need rectangular cages to provide flying room, with bars three-eighths of an inch apart to prevent escape or injury.

Imagine how you'd feel if you found your bird with its head stuck between the bars because they were too far apart.

Canaries also need more length than width in a cage. The bars should be five-eighths of an inch apart. Some finches who are as large as canaries may live in canary cages.

Budgerigars, who climb as well as fly, will be happiest in tall cages. With extra room for showing off and horizontal bars to make climbing easier for them, they will be more entertaining as pets. Cages with horizontal bars are designed for climbing birds; the cage should have one side with vertical bars to hold cups and feeders. A budgie will make a second home of a playground with swings and ladders that hang from a curtain rod.

Cockatiels and parrots, with their strong bills, need heavy metal bars on their cages. A cockatiel I kept for a friend used its cage to make noise. He ran his bill up and down the bars until it seemed as if they would wear thin. Parrots like to chew wood. A parrot on display in a sports store chewed a hole in the wooden cage beside him that nearly let the finches escape. Parrots walk a lot, strutting around the bottom of their cages, but they climb too, so they need plenty of space. If a parrot is confined in too small a cage, it becomes moody, bored, and noisy. A parrot cage should be at least six inches wider than the width of the bird with its wings outstretched.

When choosing a cage, look not only at its size in relation to the bird, but at how much room the bird will have between the perches. You can tell if a cage is large enough by snapping a perch at the end of the cage and letting your bird try it out. The bird's head shouldn't hit the roof nor should its tail touch the sides when it

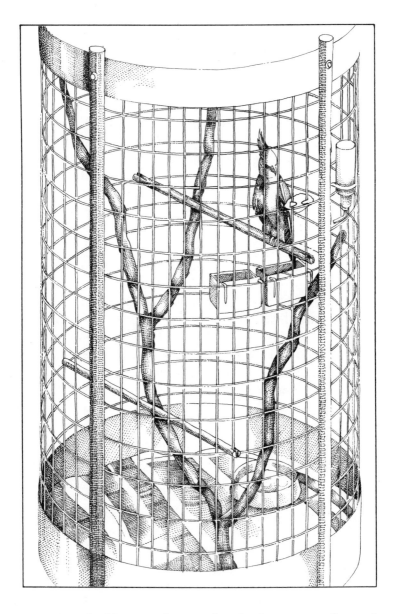

An easy-to-build aviary for a cockatiel where it may flap and climb about

sits on the perches. It should have room to flap its wings three or four times when it flies from one perch to the other.

As soon as you take a new cage home, sterilize it in boiling water or dunk it in a tubful of water, soap, and bleach. Even though a cage is new, it might have been contaminated in transit or in the store. It is even more important to sterilize an old cage, because a bird probably died in it before it was stored away.

If you plan to keep your bird in an aviary, you may use your new cage as temporary quarters. The aviary may be one purchased from a store, a simple one you make by yourself, or an elaborate one involving help from other people. More spacious than a cage, it may be equipped with toys and climbing apparatus for a psittacine and still leave room for flying and aerial acrobatics. It should have plants (real or plastic) to serve as swings, perches, and hiding places for finches, canaries, or budgies. It may house one bird or a collection.

A mixed group of birds in an aviary creates a slice of nature indoors. The aviary may include singing finches, a budgie to play the clown if it doesn't taunt the other birds, and a smiling, stomping button quail that keeps to itself on the floor. Such a mixture makes for exciting listening and watching and teaches you a great deal about birds' habits in the wild. If a pair of birds breeds and raises young, those babies will give you a proud feeling. Birds nest more readily in an aviary than in a cage, so it is the best way for an amateur to start a breeding project.

Constant exercise in an aviary keeps birds healthy by toning their muscles. It also burns off fat, so there is less danger from overeating rich food. Though you intend to give a bird in a cage a chance to fly free every day, it may be difficult to carry out this ambition when you stay late after school or spend a night with a friend. A bird in an aviary, however, has the chance to exercise every day.

Directions on how to build several different types of aviaries will be found in the appendix. The easiest and cheapest—made of wire mesh—takes little skill to bend into shape. It isn't difficult to make one out of an unfinished bookcase, either. The aviary described by Michael Shays sounds complex, but he designed it with his twelve-year-old daughter in mind when she was taking shop at school. He made sure it could be built by someone her age. When complete it looks professional, will last for years, and has enough room for one or several birds. The appendix even has plans for a heavy metal cage—the type needed for a cockatiel.

Wire mesh on the sides of aviaries should be one-fourth inch size for finches, one-half inch for budgies and canaries, and a heavy-duty mesh with larger holes for cockatiels. The roof should be solid metal or plywood so a bird will not dash against it when flying in panic.

When decorating an aviary, watch for trouble spots. Some birds seem to have a knack for slipping toenails into the loops of wire holding perches. They may also catch their leg bands on exposed prongs of metal. A bird can hang to death by a leg band or toenail. Birds bustle with curiosity, investigating the smallest escape holes, and fluttering into hiding places they cannot leave. You cannot think the way a bird does in order to close all ways of escape, but you can twist wires too tight for their toenails and bend the edges of mesh to the outside to protect them.

Commercial aviaries may be bought at some suppliers and pet stores. For a small bird—a finch, budgie, or canary—a flight cage serves as an aviary.

Once when we had a garden room with over a hundred plants in it, my husband and I turned it into an aviary. We didn't plan it that way, but when the first orange-cheeked waxbill escaped from its cage, it was soon followed by its three brothers. The birds stayed among the plants without artificial barriers to keep them there. If no such room exists in your house, perhaps part of a sunny room could be screened off with wire mesh to create a natural aviary.

Whatever size aviary you have, add some plants to make the birds feel at home. They like to bounce on springy branches, scratch in the dirt, and nibble on the leaves. They find wonderful nesting and roosting sites. In our garden-room aviary the birds hid so well in the ivy, only a hint of color here and there betrayed them. Even bushes and trees such as forsythia, honeysuckle, and wild plum will grow in an aviary if there is enough light.

The ratio of birds to plants has to weigh heavily on the plant side, however, or the birds will strip off all the leaves. Tough plants such as rubber plants, orchids, amaryllis, and large-leafed begonias withstand birds' beaks best. Ferns and small begonias are too delicate. Others taste too good. My green singing finches demolished a Christmas cactus in one day. The zebra finches ate the African violets. My lavender finches seem to take delight in watching leaves float to the floor, while the parrotlets systematically strip a branch of every green shoot from the tip to the stalk.

Sometimes the problem is temporary, because birds devour plants eagerly at first, then seem to have their fill of them. One zoo had to replace its entire planting in a new aviary, but the birds didn't destroy it a second time. Birds may be diverted from eating plants if foods they like better, such a millet sprays, lettuce, cucumber, and sprouting grass are supplied abundantly.

Before introducing plants to an aviary, check that none are poisonous to birds. Cornell University publishes a pamphlet on poisonous plants, and many gardening books describe plants that are harmful to eat. Plants for an aviary also need to be clean of insecticides. Never spray plants to kill bugs, because the birds eat insects. The soil, too, may contain something harmful to birds. Wash the entire plant in soap and water and rinse it. Then repot it in sterilized soil, which is done by soaking the soil in water and baking it in the oven at three hundred degrees for two hours. (It takes three minutes in a microwave oven.) To avoid the smell of the soil as it bakes, be sure it is covered to the surface, but not above it, with water. The flowerpots should be soaked overnight in soapy water, rinsed, then baked at two hundred seventy-five degrees for one hour.

Artificial plants are easier to clean and less likely to be chewed than real ones. Hook-bills will chew on artificial leaves but usually cannot harm tough plants, palms, or ivy. One or two types of greenery look less artificial in an aviary than a variety. A tree limb decorated with small clumps of leaves or flowers adds color and realism.

Plants may be used in cages, too; artificial ones last much longer than living ones. Caged birds tend to be more bored and never outgrow nibbling on anything in the cage that will divert them. Artificial plants should be washed weekly in soap, water, and bleach; living plants need soap and water—no bleach—and they should be rinsed clean.

All birds like a place to hide in a cage as well as in an aviary. They also like to play on anything around. Budgie and parrot toys add interest to their lives. But flying and climbing room count most of all. The smaller the space, the fewer diversions it will hold and still leave room for flight. This makes an aviary one of the best gifts you can give your bird.

5

CAGE EQUIPMENT

A cage usually comes equipped with a few perches and seed and water cups. Many changes will be needed before the cage makes a perfect home for your bird. These involve extra feeders, a bath, and different types of perches.

In addition to the cups fastened to the cage add an Oasis or Hartz ball-bearing water bottle and a glass or plastic tube feeder for seed. The water bottle is exactly like the ones sold for hamsters and rabbits. In fact a hamster bottle is better than the type sold especially for birds because the plastic is clear, letting you see if it stays clean. These bottles keep water fresh and clean better than any other feeder.

Tube feeders come in two parts: a tube to hold water or seed and a lip section to fit between the cage bars. A tube with a wide diameter is better than a narrow one because it holds more seed and clogs less easily. The tight bars of the cage rather than a clip hold one type of feeder in place. This feeder has a deep lip, but as a seed feeder, it can kill a bird. Once when caring for a friend's zebra finch, I noticed the bird pecking savagely at such a feeder. Later it looked sick. I tossed a handful of seed on the cage floor, and the finch ate hungrily. Within an hour it was hopping about happily again. The finch's conical bill was too fat to fit into the narrow opening of the feeder, so it had been starving. This type of feeder can be used successfully for water, however.

Tube feeders should be put together according to the directions on the packages or they won't work properly. Different brands do not have interchangeable parts and will clog or leak if mixed up. Any feeder clogs from strange items mixed in the seed, such as sunflower seed, webs from seed caterpillars, droppings from birds, or a splash of water. You can tell the seed is flowing properly if the level of the feeder drops during the day.

The cups for budgies, parrots, and cockatiels should be mounted *inside* the cage because hook-bills dislike poking their heads into small holes to reach seed or water. Since parrots and cockatiels play with their dishes, pick heavy containers if you don't want the contents scattered. Finches and canaries, however, will poke into anything and will find seed even when the cups are mounted outside the cage. Cups and dishes that won't harm birds are made of plastic, metal (not galvanized), glass, or glazed ceramic ware. Hooded ones keep out bird droppings, which helps keep the seed and water clean.

When you need to add a new dish to a hook-bill's cage, you will discover how much this bird dislikes change. At first my cockatiel, Scratch-it, wouldn't even walk close to a new dish. It took three weeks before he would touch treats in it. So when you buy a new bird and want it to eat properly, you should give it familiar seed cups. In time, however, it will accept almost any type of feeder.

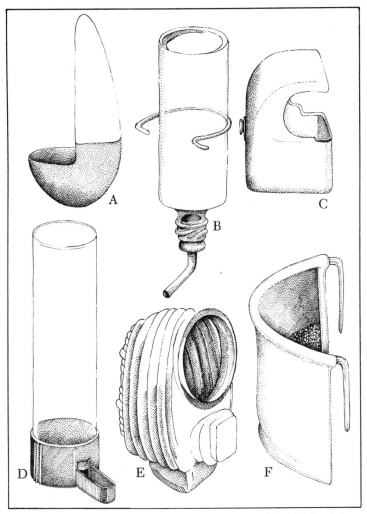

Feeders: a) Water feeder (don't use it for seed for finches)
b) Water stays cleanest in this feeder.
c) Hooded cup
d) The best tube feeder (water or seed)
e) Cup for canaries or finches
f) Use heavy-duty, open-top cups for psittacines.
Note: Use *two* water and *two* seed cups or tubes in every cage.

A wild-bird feeder makes an attractive and time-saving addition to an aviary or large cage. An inexpensive one that has a tray designed to prevent birds from tossing seed hither and thither is an E-Z-FIL. Even my budgie and parrotlets eat on one without chewing it, and the finches share it with each other with a minimum of pushing. Some of the finches like to sleep on the rim.

In an aviary food may be served in saucers placed in sheltered locations where droppings won't land on top of the seed. Ground-feeding birds easily locate food in saucers.

A plastic kitchen drawer divider can hold fruits, vegetables, and scrambled eggs in an aviary. It keeps the food clean, and the high edges prevent the birds from scattering it all over the floor.

You may have to use your own ingenuity to solve feeding problems. I once found a baby button quail in a saucer of seed. Every time he tried to climb up the slippery side, he tumbled in again, head over heels. A soap dish with an eighth-inch-high edge held the seed, but let the baby quail climb out. A water bottle with a nozzle will keep nectar fresh and clean for a soft-billed bird.

Avoid using unglazed dishes for water, because they leak. And don't be tempted by tuna cans, which may seem a handy size for seed; they rust, and the galvanized metal, when new, might poison the bird.

The cleverer you are at placing feeders, the less soiled the food in them becomes. A tube feeder mounted over the end of a perch stays clean even if a bird hops on it. Such feeders need to be near the bottom of the cage to control flying chaff, but water feeders can be high in the cage where they have less chance of collecting droppings. A bird once proved me wrong, however, by roosting on the lip of the feeder because it was the highest perch in the cage. As soon as I gave him a higher perch, he stopped dirtying the feeder. Of course, water bottles may be located anywhere in the cage, since the water inside stays clean. Feeders at both the top and bottom of a cage or aviary have the added advantage of encouring birds to exercise.

Besides water and seed cups, cages come equipped with dowel perches of various lengths. These perches should be made of soft wood for finches and canaries and of hardwood for hook-bills. Canary perches should be flat on top. A perch is the right size for a bird if its toes do not meet underneath it, yet circle both sides. The trouble with dowel perches is that they are too even, too round and often too small for a bird's feet.

Branches from trees or bushes make better perches than ones you buy in stores. However, keep the two short dowel perches that fit in front of the seed cups, because branches won't fit there. It is always fun to please a pet, and a bird shows its delight by tasting the branches, hunting for insects, and nibbling on the tips. They enjoy the springy feel of branches—the rough surface files their toenails, and the varying thicknesses give exercise to the muscles of the feet as they grip them. When choosing branches, pick those with limbs branching off the main stem; this gives a thick base and smaller and smaller twigs to create different sized perches. Forsythia and honeysuckle have springy, multibranching limbs the right size for small birds. Willow, apple, oak, and other fruit and hardwood trees fit the feet of all sizes of birds, and psittacines can eat them safely. Avoid hemlock and yew or any trees and bushes that might be poisonous.

Neighbors dislike seeing their hedges and parks plundered for branches, however, so be careful when you go perch-hunting. Since many trees are sprayed to kill pests,

Compare the size of a cockatiel (*top*), finch (*bottom*), and canary (*right*). Canaries may chase finches; if they do, then they cannot live together.

wash all branches thoroughly. Wait until they are dry before using them, because wet perches are dangerous to a bird's health. If you keep a supply of limbs on hand, a dry one will always be ready to replace dirty ones.

It's best to arrange perches—and toys—at the ends of a cage rather than down the middle, which cuts off a bird's flying space. This same general arrangement applies to aviaries as well.

A rug for the floor of the cage or aviary can be made of a variety of materials. The cheapest and most common is a sheet of newspaper, which folds up the chaff and droppings neatly. Use newspapers a week or more old so the ink has dried and won't come off on a bird's feet. There's a risk of lead poisoning from the ink if it sticks to a bird's toes and is eaten.

Birds sometimes use newspapers on the floor for their own purposes. One budgie rolls his ball around under the newspaper. There's a cockatiel who seems to feel more secure when he sleeps under his paper. Only once did I have trouble with newspapers as a floor covering. I had tried to save time by placing a layer of five or six papers in the cage. A baby zebra finch crawled beneath the pile and could not lift what to him was a heavy load and would have died if he had not been found in time.

Astroturf looks like a lawn if it is used for the floor of an aviary. The chaff and droppings sink between the blades, giving the aviary a clean look, and the droppings can be vacuumed out of it each week. Linoleum may also be used as a floor covering.

Gravel papers sold for birds *hurt their feet*. Only parrots and game birds who have tough feet, can walk on sand in the bottom of their cages. Unfortunately sand picks up odors, so it must be changed frequently. Parrot cages sometimes have grills at the bottom, but they dislike walking on them and become frustrated when their favorite toys fall underneath.

Grilled bottoms work better for soft-billed birds because they make a mess of everything. The grills, however, need to be cleaned thoroughly every few days. Since soft-billed birds eat off the floor, placing clean newspapers on top of the floor twice a day is still the easiest way to keep the cage clean.

Birds love to take baths, so while you are buying equipment, choose a birdbath. A dish on the floor works just as well, but birdbaths have hoods which keep most of the flying drops inside. The bottom of the bath should be a solid color or the bird cannot gauge the depth of the water and refuses to go in. If saucers are used instead of baths, they should be glazed ceramicware or opaque glass. In my aviary four or five finches take communal baths in a large shallow soup bowl. An eight-inch flowerpot saucer holds enough water for a bath-loving mynah or cockatiel.

The secret to a sweet-smelling cage is cleanliness. A bird has no odor. Odor comes from a large accumulation of droppings or from water soaking into droppings or fallen seed. The paper in the bottom of the cage will need changing at least two or three times a week, if not every day. You can cut a week's supply at once, then remove the top piece each day. Whenever it becomes damp it will need changing. Perches are a bird's bed, couch, napkin, and even its launching pad and springboard, so they should be scraped clean whenever they need it. Water containers should be cleaned every day by rubbing them hard with your finger to take away the slimly feel inside, and then washing and rinsing them.

Once a week mix up a sterilizing solution in a laundry tub or the kitchen sink. Fill it with hot water, then add soap or detergent and a quarter cup of bleach. Everything your bird uses should be washed in this solution. Have a bottle brush just for your bird so you won't touch one belonging to the family.

Wash the bird's food dishes first when the water is cleanest. The water bottle needs special attention. Algae, a greenish film, collects around the top of the bottle where the spout screws on. A bent bottle brush will reach the algae and clean it off. The algae can be killed by soaking the bottle *full* to the top with water and bleach. Rinse it before refilling it. Then wash the other tube feeders (including those for seed) and the cups. The seed feeders must be completely dry before being refilled with seed or the seed will spoil.

Next wash the perches and set them aside to dry.

Finally, dunk the entire cage in the washing solution and brush off any clinging dirt. If you use Astroturf, soak it for an hour or overnight. Then bang it free of debris on a rock or sidewalk and let it dry.

Cleanliness and clean water every day are probably the two most important items in keeping your bird healthy. The sterilizing solution is your best protection against pests, too.

6

WHERE TO PUT
THE CAGE

A new home full of love and attention transforms a bird from a flighty creature to an affectionate pet. But its future depends on many things. A bird will stay alive and feel more comfortable with its cage in the right place in the right room. Nature protects wildlife outdoors. An American goldfinch in the wild, for example, has a thousand more feathers in the winter than in the summer. But a caged bird, unless it is raised in an outdoor aviary, will not fare as well as its wild cousin when the temperature changes; you must protect it.

Drafts are probably the principal bird killer. A cage in a drafty place will soon hold a dead bird. Air currents can be treacherous. Drafts bounce off windows when warm air from the room hits the cool glass or when cold air from outside seeps around the edges of the window. Storm windows help keep out these killer air currents, and putty packed around the edges of windows, or tape on the seams, will cut drafts. Crosscurrents of air may move between doors and open windows and along hallways or may simply be caused by hot air rising.

Even in warm weather birds feel drafts from open windows and doors. When a window is open near a bird, protect it by draping a towel over one end of the cage or by enclosing both ends and the back of the cage. If a bird must live in a room with an air conditioner, place the cage as far as possible from the unit.

One way to locate a safe place to put your bird is to hold a lighted candle in the area where you would like the cage. If the flame burns steadily without wavering, the area is safe. Usually you will find a spot a foot or two on either side of a window or in a corner of the room. By testing an aviary the same way you will learn if one end or the back needs a protective screen of plastic or glass to stop a draft.

A temperature that feels comfortable to a person usually feels comfortable to a bird, too. A bird bears cold fairly easily because it can fluff its feathers to trap air between them, which acts as insulation. If it is hot, a bird pants. A room may be as cool as forty-five to fifty degrees F (eight to eleven C) and as hot as sixty-five to seventy degrees F (eighteen or twenty-one C) without affecting a bird. When the thermometer goes into the eighties F (about twenty-seven degrees C), try to find a cool spot for your bird. The solution may be a cooling unit, open windows, or a cooler room downstairs.

A sudden change in temperature affects a bird more than cold or heat. The temperature often changes rapidly in the kitchen or near radiators. A kitchen seems a good place for a bird, but the room has all sorts of disadvantages. The temperature changes more than ten degrees in an hour when someone starts cooking. Empty pans left on hot burners so they reach high temperatures can kill a bird. I knew a man who left a pan cooking until it ran dry and burned; his entire collection of birds died.

A kitchen is humid. Over a period of time high humidity affects a bird's feathers so they may break off. Even a damp room in a garage or basement may injure a bird. However, a garage or basement floor and walls may be covered with heavy plastic or waterproof paint so they cease to sweat, thus making the rooms safe for your pet.

Birds need ventilation to survive. Small or tightly closed quarters like attics often lack cross-ventilation. If a room becomes smoggy with cigarette smoke, it affects a bird even more than it does people. Its small lungs cannot cope with it. Even one person smoking by the cage can cause trouble.

A bird sings a joyous greeting to the outdoors when its cage is set on a porch. Many houses especially in the South have outdoor living areas—swimming pools, patios, miniature gardens, environment rooms. A bird may live safely in these areas as long as they are screened-in so predators—like the neighbor's cat—can't reach them.

These areas can be filled with sunshine. One day when I glanced into the aviary, I noticed the crimson pileated finch lying on its side. All its feathers stuck out at angles and its crest stood up straight. It was panting. Nothing was wrong. It was just enjoying a sunbath. A few minutes later it flew into the shade behind the wall to cool off. The important item—shade—made it possible for the bird to enjoy the sun and survive. If your bird is exposed to direct sunlight on a porch or by an open window, cover one end of the cage with a sheet or towel to provide shade.

Any outdoor living area or aviary should be constructed to give a bird shelter from rain, wind, and storms as well as from the sun. At night especially a bird needs a retreat. In the North it is safer to let birds come into the house at night because even in summer the temperature can drop suddenly. Outdoor aviaries face a constant danger from pests—rats, snakes, mosquitoes, and cats.

The practice of putting a bird outside on pleasant days can be more harmful than helpful. Once a bird is adjusted to living inside, he should not be forced to make quick adjustments to outside, which has different temperature, humidity, and sounds.

Other pets should not be allowed to bother a bird. A girl I know kept her zebra finch in a room where the cat couldn't go. But one day someone left the door open. The cat seized the bird. After being chased all over the house by the girl's father, the cat finally dropped the finch unharmed. Four years later the door was left open again, and the cat killed the bird.

Hang the cage from the ceiling away from furniture to safeguard it from a cat's leap. The top of a bookcase is usually high enough to discourage a dog. Narrow bars, immovable seed cups, a clip on the door of the cage make it mouse-proof. The bottom of a cage should be wired so the tray won't fall out if the cage tips over. An aviary, because it is enclosed, is safest—provided the door cannot be shoved open. Birds who become escape artists, especially parrots, may need a metal lock on the door to keep them safe when you are away. A friend of mine discovered combination locks were essential. Before she used locks, the parrots kept getting out and teasing her dogs!

Once you have learned to keep your other pets away from your bird and have located a draft-free place for its cage, you will know it is safe even when you are away. Then you may look forward to hours of enjoyment with it when you come home.

7

WHAT TO FEED YOUR BIRD FOR HEALTH AND HAPPINESS

PART I:
BASIC FOODS

A bird needs four basic foods to stay alive: seed, water, gravel, and cuttlebone. A few birds live indefinitely on this diet, but most also need extra foods such as vegetables and greens. When you bring your bird home, prepare the cage with the basic foods before putting your bird inside. Then it won't go through minutes of panic while you fasten the feeding cups in place. It will quickly spot the fresh seed and water, take a taste, and say thank you with a happy peep.

Fresh water is a bird's most important food. Water feeders should be washed and refilled every day. If your community has problems with water, you might try boiling the tap water and storing a jar of it in the refrigerator, but let it reach room temperature before you put it into the cage. A spring or well almost always has pure water.

When you first buy a bird and whenever you move to a new location, you can use bottled water for the first few days. This way, though other things may upset your bird, you will know the drinking water has not caused problems.

When you understand the way a bird digests its food, you'll know why it always needs full seed cups. Birds have a high rate of metabolism. This is the process by which they break down food and turn it into energy. They use up energy quickly by flying and hopping about. Because they keep their bodies as light as possible for flight, most species are highly selective in their diet and won't eat food they cannot digest rapidly.

Birds do not have teeth. Their taste glands are scanty and they tend to bolt their food without tasting or moistening it before swallowing. The digestive tube from the back of a bird's mouth to its stomach has a pouch called the crop. It is a bit like a balloon in the middle of a bird's throat. The crop is used to store food when a bird eats faster than it can digest its food. When it sleeps or rests, it digests whatever is left in the crop. Since birds digest food rapidly and can store only tiny amounts in their crops, they eat almost constantly. They face hunger and starvation if food is not available in their cages all the time.

A bird's stomach is usually divided into two parts. One is small and begins the breakdown of the food. The other part is the gizzard, which acts as a grinding machine. Its walls crush and grind hard materials like seed, often with the aid of grit for an abrasive. The right kind of grit supplies valuable minerals, such as calcium and phosphorous, needed especially for bone and feather development. Wild birds use all sorts of things for grit. An ornithology class in its study of birds found bits of sand (some so fine it felt smooth as silver polish), sea shells, bones, and even pieces of metal in birds' gizzards.

Almost all birds, wild ones as well as tame ones, need grit. Grit for pets is boxed as "bird gravel." The commercial grit consists of ground quartz with oyster shell and trace minerals. Sometimes it contains charcoal to prevent food from souring while it is digested. Grit keeps indefinitely.

The grit sold for birds has gone through a sterilizing and cleaning process. If you were to pick sand from the seashore or backyard, it wouldn't have the extra ingredients or the cleanliness of commercial grit. It could be the wrong size, too. Small birds use tiny pieces of grit sold as canary gravel. Budgies and cockatiels eat a coarser kind—packaged as budgerigar (or parakeet) gravel. Budgies should not have charcoal in their gravel. A finch should have canary, not budgerigar, gravel.

Birds will peck fresh grit as eagerly as a treat. After it reaches their gizzards, it wears down into such tiny pieces it passes out through the intestines. This is why they need a constant supply.

For years most people tossed grit on the bottom of the cage—the worst possible place for it. It gives birds sore feet and picks up dirt from the floor. A small cup of grit on the side of the cage stays clean. Stir it with your finger to keep it soft, add a bit on top when you change the cage, and replace the whole cupful once a week. You may be surprised to find out how much your bird enjoys it.

The third basic food, cuttlebone, comes from the cuttlefish, a squidlike sea mollusk with a hard internal shell. The bone is white with a hard, glossy, shell-like back and a round, soft front. The soft side should face the bird. It helps birds in two ways: they sharpen their bills on it, and they get calcium from it. Cuttlebones should be fresh, for then they are soft. Your fingernail sinks easily into a fresh one. The ones sold in some pet stores and supermarkets and those found in old cages tend to be hard and dry. Soft, fresh ones may be bought from suppliers or from a store that sells them by the pound. Ones sold by weight are usually fresh. Pieces work just as well as whole ones. A bird needs a new cuttlebone whenever it eats away the soft part of its current one, or if the bone becomes hard. It should be replaced every month or two.

The fourth basic food—seed—comes in many varieties. Finch seed mixtures contain various millets, a round, red millet and panicum, a small, round, yellow seed, as well as a flat, oval seed known as canary seed. Canaries eat canary seed and rape seed, a tiny, black seed. Budgies like a mixture with white proso millet, which is larger than panicum, some canary seed, and a small amount of oats. Lovebirds, cockatiels, and other parakeets live well on the budgie mixture plus sunflower or safflower seeds. Complete diets for a large variety of birds will be found in the appendix.

A great deal of research has gone into the preparation of seed mixtures for different species of birds. A finch cannot live well on a budgie mixture, nor a canary on finch seed. When a friend of mine left her finches with a bird-sitter, the woman substituted wild bird seed when she ran out of finch seed. She felt sure some of the seeds would keep the birds alive. Although she bought finch seed the next evening, during the night half the finches died. A substitute diet never works for long.

The correct diet prolongs a bird's life. The molting period puts great stress on a bird's body when it must produce a whole new set of feathers. You can help it most by providing a good, complete diet year round so your pet is in top condition to withstand the extra demands of molting. No amount of molting food—a commercial product on the market—will replace in a week or two what has been lacking for a year.

Fresh seed, like pure water, is a health insurance. The food value is higher and your bird likes the taste better; hence, it eats more. Fresh seed will sprout and grow. You can test it yourself. Take four or five thicknesses of paper toweling, wet them, and wring out the excess water, leaving the towels moist. Sprinkle a few seeds on one side of the papers; fold the other side of the towel over them. Then place the wrapped seeds in a plastic bag to keep them moist and set the packet in a warm place. Within a day or two the seeds will double in size and sprout into light green shoots. Sometimes good seed fails to sprout because it is too wet or dry. Try sprouting it two or three times before deciding it is too old to feed your bird.

It can also be tested for freshness by tasting it yourself: it should have a sweet, nut-like flavor. Old seed, because it has lost its oil, tastes harsh, bitter, and dried out. Another way to test seed is by the smell: it should have a sweet, pleasant odor. Moldy seed smells stale and unpleasant and can make a bird sick. Good seeds look plump and shiny. Bad seeds look dusty when poured onto a paper.

Seed with small white caterpillars in it is not bad for birds. These caterpillars hatch in seed, especially in the summer, and add protein to the bird's diet. However, if a box of seed has a large number of webs clinging to the sides, it means the caterpillars *and* the seed were there a long time. If the caterpillars should turn into moths, they can cause trouble in the house. I still remember the time I found moths in the breakfast cereal! Now I stick bay leaf in the seed to kill the caterpillars and cover the seed pails with window screening.

Reputable suppliers almost always sell fresh seed. Two or three pounds can be stored for one bird and remain fresh until used. Since a larger order costs less per pound, you might pool your order with a group of friends. Before the new seed arrives, clean the storage container with soap, water, and bleach and let it dry thoroughly before adding new seed. If the container isn't dry, the seed will turn moldy. Any leftover seed should be dumped on top so it will be used first. When the seed arrives, meet at one house, divide the spoils, and exchange bird stories at the same time.

It may seem a bother to order seed by mail, but it is so much better for a bird that all breeders recommend it. Seed in boxes at the supermarket and in most pet stores may sit around for weeks and months until no one knows how old it is. If you can find a pet, hardware, or natural food store that sells seed in bulk, it should be as fresh as when ordered directly from a supplier.

Seed stays fresh only when stored properly in a dry place. A pound or two, because it is used quickly, may be kept in a tightly closed jar or plastic bag. Larger amounts will keep for short periods of time in plastic pails or in metal ones lined with plastic bags. Since seed needs to breathe to live, air must circulate around it. It can be stored in a wooden bin similar to the ones used to keep oats for horses. If it is in a pail, the lid can be left ajar or the top covered with screen, but the seed should be stirred occasionally to expose it to the air. Buy new seed often —about every three months.

A bird should have all the fresh seed it wants. Just

filling the feeders doesn't guarantee it will have enough. If you have watched a bird eat, you know how it cracks the seed first, then lets the husk dribble down on whatever lies below. A seed dish can easily acquire a layer of husks. A smart bird whisks them off with its bill to find the good seed underneath. Blow the chaff off the seed whenever you fill the dish. Since the chaff may mix into the seed, empty the seed cups twice a week and refill them with all new seed. A tube feeder will not need changing, but watch the lip for a collection of chaff, and be sure the *level* in the feeder drops during the day to prove the bird is eating.

A hook-bill may open its beak in anger when you touch its dish. Parrots will even attack a hand in their cages. Tap on the roof of the cage to distract the bird long enough for you to clean off the surface of the seed or to replace the dish.

It helps to know what a bird *has been* eating, because it is more likely to eat familiar foods than something new. Don't make big changes in diet the first few days, because the bird may refuse to eat the strange new food. Only if the seed has been the wrong kind should you make any substitutions. A family with a new cockatiel discovered it had previously lived on finch seed alone. It needed a budgie mixture and sunflower or safflower seeds. The right seed should be mixed half and half with the old seed the first day. Increase the amount of the right seed every day until by the end of the week the bird has only the right seed in its feeder.

Sunflower seed has some problems connected with feeding it to birds. It is narcotic, which is bad for a bird's system. Safflower seed can be gradually substituted for sunflower seed if a bird can be made to accept it. The change cannot be made abruptly without harming the bird, since it still needs some of the nutrients of the sunflower seed. This is why many breeders are moving toward nutrient diets which contain all the supplements necessary for the larger hook-bills.

Sometimes people worry because their birds throw so much seed out of their cups. The birds are hunting for favorite seeds. In the wild a bird might fly fifty miles to find a seed it needs in its diet, but in a cage all it needs to do is empty the seed cup. It will probably clean up most of the mess, but whatever remains at paper-changing time will make a feast for the wild birds out-doors.

The basic foods should be explained to everyone in the family and the bird-sitter if you go away. When I was twelve, I had a canary at summer camp and, lured out-doors by horses and crayfish, I forgot the canary one day. When I came in after dinner, he was dead. I saw why: both the seed and water cups were empty. That's a high price to pay for forgetting. A canary can starve to death in twenty-four hours. It doesn't take much longer to starve a heartier bird, since they all have such high metabolism.

It is important to have a routine. Feed your bird every day before breakfast when you are hungry, too. The feeders should be checked two or three times a day —before school, after school, after dinner, or whenever is best for you. Bedtime is a poor time because the bird cannot eat in the dark. It takes only five minutes to feed a bird. Even with thirty or more birds in my aviary it takes only fifteen minutes for the morning feeding. It would be less than that if it didn't take so long to prepare food for my soft-billed birds. Your bird will like having a routine, too, and will watch eagerly for the sight of you each morning.

PART II:
EXTRA FOODS COMPLETE THE DIET

Birds seem to be conservative by nature. Once they learn to eat one type of food, they object to a change. A wise owner exposes his bird to as many different types of food as possible while it is young—not all at once, but bit by bit. Other birds who already like the foods teach newcomers to eat them, but a single bird relies on its owner for training.

Some of the extra foods for birds are just as necessary as their basic seed mixture. Few birds live easily on only seed. If you wonder if a food is healthy for birds, check the list at the back of the book.

The extra foods, often called supplements, keep a bird's diet varied. They should be fed in the morning because soft foods like greens, vegetables, insects, and so forth, spoil easily. They should be removed long before dark, otherwise they might be eaten late and remain undigested in the bird's crop overnight. A bird feels more comfortable at night if its crop is empty.

Birds need small amounts of the extra foods. A caged bird should have only the amount of greens or fruit it cleans up in a half hour each day. Birds in aviaries, who have more exercise, may have more extra foods, provided none are left long enough to spoil. All these foods should be fresh and washed thoroughly.

Birds would find a salad bar at a restaurant a great treat. The various types of greens and the raw vegetables and tomatoes would appeal to them. The freshest greens for your bird will be the ones your family eats, because greens tend to wilt if kept around too long. Those with dark green leaves have the most vitamins and minerals.

Wild edibles

For example, romaine lettuce makes a far better food than iceberg lettuce, which is largely water. Spinach is one of the richest sources of vitamins. It is also sprayed less during the growing season, so is less likely to have a residue of insecticides on it than other vegetables. You may feed other greens such as kale, comfrey, endive, and the leafy tops of root vegetables like carrots, beets, and turnips. Parsley, however, may be fatal to birds.

If a bird could do its own food gathering in the backyard or fields, it would snap up all sorts of greens and seeds you might not even think of picking for it. Chickweed, for example, a pest to most gardeners, is a treat to birds and one of the healthiest foods it can eat. In spring chickweed sprinkles lawns and roadsides with tiny blue flowers—an easy time of year to recognize it. Birds like the flowers, the seeds when they come out, and even the stems.

Dandelion leaves, especially the tender, young ones, make excellent greens for birds. Birds like clover leaves and flowers that have gone to seed. Even fresh grass clippings make greens for birds. Have you ever noticed how wild birds congregate on some lawns after mowing? Every summer, when I bring a handful of wild grasses into the aviary, the lavender finches, orange-cheeked waxbills, and canary leave every other food to rummage in the treat. Sometimes they look first for seeds on the wild grasses; sometimes they pinch the stems to extract the juice. Your bird will develop a preference for some grass you pick and look for it eagerly throughout the growing season.

Hook-bills have a special need for greens. The limbs of trees and bushes contain cellulose, which hook-bills must have in their diet. In the wild, budgies live mainly on wild grasses, limbs, and bark. But finches, too, nibble the tips of green branches, and all birds like budding branches in the springtime. Forsythia and honeysuckle especially, when the tiny buds gleam in their shields, will be gobbled by birds. Willow, fruit, and nut trees all have bird-pleasing flavors. The 8 in 1 Woodland Mix for budgies has bark in it for those who cannot find tree limbs. But keep a wary eye out for anything that might be poisonous to birds and pick only greens you recognize. To be safe, wash the wild ones, too.

You can also grow your own greens indoors. How birds enjoy tiny blades two or three inches tall! Fill a few flowerpots with dirt bought at a store (not from outdoors where it can be contaminated with sprays), or use vermiculite or peat moss. Sprinkle some easy-to-grow seeds like millet, alfalfa, lettuce, celery, or your bird seed *on top* of the soil. The seeds will grow more quickly if the moisture stays in, so cover the pots with plastic wrap tightened around the tops with rubber bands. The saucers under the pots need to stay full of water for the seeds to sprout. Extra light from a window, fluorescent light, or table lamp speeds the germination. If you rotate three or four flowerpots of grass, your bird will have a continuous supply. It's a delight to watch a brightly colored bird sitting among the green blades slipping a piece of grass through its bill. Some birds, like Gouldian finches, nest more readily if they have tender grass to eat.

Many breeders feed soaked seed, but it spoils so quickly it is wiser to begin with grasses. The best way to sprout seeds is described in the appendix.

Millet sprays with the seeds still on the stalk almost rank as a basic food because birds enjoy them so much. This treat harks back to when their wild ancestors picked their own seeds off the stem. A budgie should always have a fresh millet spray in its cage. The sprays will be fresh if ordered from a supplier or a farm that grows them. Boxed ones too often contain old, dry seeds with little nutritional value.

Breeders recommend carrots more often than any other vegetable. Grate them for finches and canaries, chop them for budgies, and cut them in strips for larger hookbills. Grated carrots and cooked eggs may be fed as a nestling food (an easy-to-digest food) to baby birds.

Old, fat cucumbers—but not overripe ones—have lots of seeds, which are a bird's favorite part of a slice. Green pepper seeds have a high food value. Among other vegetables helpful to birds are broccoli (cooked or raw), steamed squash (the yellower the better), and mashed sweet or white potatoes (well-suited for sick or weak birds). Corn on the cob makes a treat birds like, though other vegetables have priority. My Gouldian finches and button quail like the corn silk better than the corn. Frozen vegetables (thawed) may be substituted for fresh ones.

Birds seem to enjoy fruits the way people do. Fruits have the same nutritional value as vegetables, so both make good foods as long as they are fresh, ripe, and without spoiled spots. Oranges (and grapefruits) may be one of the few fruits available year round in your state. Cut them cartwheel fashion across the sections to make it easy for a bird to rip out the pulp. Melons make a sweet treat, but remove them within an hour in hot weather, because they spoil quickly. Wild berries—strawberries, raspberries, blackberries, currants, blueberries—that you eat yourself make easy-to-bite treats. Stick to berries you know so you don't feed a poisonous one by mistake. Grapes have a high protein value, so ration them to birds in cages. Apples, low on the ladder for food value but easily available, should be cut in wedges.

Fruit: A delicious and healthful treat

The most important part of feeding greens, vegetables, and fruits is washing them. Whether they came from the supermarket or the backyard, they can be contaminated with insecticides. Soak all greens a few minutes first, then rinse and rinse them. Remove all wilted or spoiled leaves. Grapes wash clean in water, but the stems may retain insecticides, so remove the grapes when giving them to a bird. All fruits and vegetables should be clean, unspoiled, and firm.

Live food forms a natural part of the diet for wild birds. It is probably the most difficult part of the diet to replace in captivity. Some substitute is essential for soft-billed birds and is needed by almost all species at breeding time. Most birds stay healthier with live food (or a substitute) as part of their daily diet. A bird's need for live food may be supplied by mealworms, an insectile mixture, hens' eggs, or bugs—beetles, spiders, flies, and so forth.

Usually eggs in some form make the easiest substitute. Through the years I have found scrambled eggs have the most advantages for feeding in small quantities. For a single bird beat four eggs with a half tablespoon of milk until they are well mixed. Use a half tablespoon or less of butter in the frying pan and cook the eggs until they are dry. If they are not cooked thoroughly, the eggs will spoil when given to a bird. Let the scrambled eggs cool. Then wrap them in teaspoon-size packets with plastic wrap and store them in the freezer. Thaw the eggs for a few minutes before feeding them to your bird, especially if feeding delicate birds such as canaries. In an aviary the frozen chunks are quickly broken up by the birds.

Many breeders mash hard-boiled eggs, or the yolks only, for birds with chicks in the nest—but the eggs cannot be left more than a couple of hours without spoiling. The room temperature should be sixty-five degrees or over when birds are fed egg to make digesting easy.

Soft-billed birds such as Pekin robins, honeycreepers, mynah birds, and lories should have eggs as part of their basic diet. Almost all other species benefit from them, but canaries should have them only when feeding their young.

Mealworms are the easiest live food to give a bird. They should be rationed to one or two a day to birds in cages unless live food forms part of the bird's basic diet; then they may have more. These small, light-colored worms may be bought at pet stores or ordered cheaply through the mail from advertisers in *American Cage Bird Magazine*. If you live in the North, order mealworms before winter or no matter how carefully they are packed, many will die in transit.

As soon as the mealworms arrive, they need to be shaken out of the newspapers in which they are packaged. Small numbers, up to five hundred, may be stored in a jar in the refrigerator. It is better to leave the jar uncovered, but if you fear it may spill, use a cap punched full of holes. Shake the jar each day when you remove worms. Otherwise they stick in the bottom and die. Mealworms packed in plastic cartons that pet stores sell may also be stored in the refrigerator in the carton as long as it has holes in the cover.

The cool temperature puts mealworms into the dormant phase of their cycle, and they will live a long time in the refrigerator. They need a little moisture every other week or so. Just drop a small piece of damp paper towel or a quarter inch wedge of apple in the container. If the mealworms become too wet, however, they will die.

Larger numbers of mealworms keep best in a steep-sided container with a deep bed of cereal. The top should be covered with mesh screen to keep out insects and to be sure no worms escape. A tight cover would cut off the air supply. Mealworms eat any cereal feed. Although barley makes the best type, bran is easier to find in feed and health food stores. H-O Oats, 100% Bran, or baby cereal also may be fed.

A mealworm culture will grow in a deep bed of cereal. They like to live in damp, dark places. It takes four to six months for mealworms to grow from larva (worm) to pupa (which looks like a short, white grub with a pointed tail) to beetle. The warmer it is, the faster they grow. The beetles lay eggs in dried bread, sawdust, burlap, or peat moss in the bottom of the culture. A few layers of burlap on top of the bran base prevents too much moisture from wetting the culture. Add apples— the cores, parings, or entire fruit—on top of the burlap. Many books recommend potatoes, but the odor is unpleasant.

Fruit flies, an even more nutritious food than mealworms, multiply swiftly in a jar containing fruit. They mature within a week in warm weather. Any jar with a hole in the top may be partially filled with fruit left to rot. Banana skins, which have little odor, make a good base. An open jar from which the flies can escape should be left near the bird, which will catch its own supply. The trouble with fruit flies is that when they leave the jar, some find their way to your kitchen and become pests.

There are other substitutes for live food. A veterinarian once surprised me by suggesting moistened dog food— something I already had at home. He said to use a high quality dog food such as Purina Dog Chow or Gaines Meal. Since it is moistened, it spoils easily, so it cannot be left more than a few hours in a cage. If it is soggy, the birds won't touch it. Button quail and some of the finches eat it dry if I grind it small enough. They also eat ground mynah food and chicken mash.

You can buy an insectivorous mixture called Bekfin manufactured by Sluis as a substitute for live food. It is imported from the Netherlands and can be ordered from suppliers in this country. Since few domestic birds in the United States have seen the mixture, your bird may be reluctant to taste it. Try mixing in a bit of honey. Once the bird learns to eat Bekfin, it not only watches for a new supply, but if it has young, feeds the mixture to them. Science Diet, a moist food for soft-bills, is distributed through some pet stores.

An insectivorous mixture can be made from equal amounts of (1) soy bean flour or powder (found among puppy products), (2) whole wheat flour (sold in health food stores), (3) coarse ground or tiny shrimp, (4) meat and bone meal, and (5) fish meal (among the products sold for fish in aquariums).

Certain species of birds, such as soft-billed finches, mynah birds, and lories, eat only soft foods. Complete diets for these birds may be found in Clive Roots's *Softbilled Birds*. Their diet consists of fruit, vegetables, egg, live food, an insectivorous mixture, and nectar. Nectar may be mixed easily with one part honey to four parts water. A large peanut butter jar with measurements on the side and a tight cap works well both for mixing and storing. The honey-water keeps in the refrigerator for a week or more. Vitamins may be added to the nectar every other day—one drop to four ounces. Always use vitamins manufactured for human babies (not those for animals and birds) because they are purer and safer. Since honey ferments quickly in a warm room, the nectar mixture needs to be changed twice a day. Avoid fats and oils in a soft-bill's menu. Cheese from which the oil has been removed by drying it out makes a good food. Lean ground meat may be added to an insectile mixture, but add it only at the last minute to prevent spoiling.

Trace minerals needed by birds come in gravel mixtures. A mineral block for budgies and other hook-bills is a good investment both for its food value and because the birds sharpen their bills on it. They chew on salt spools, too. The blocks and salt spools are too hard for canaries and finches, however, but they nibble on salt crystals sold for aquariums. Susie, my first successful zebra finch parent, used to stand teetering and slipping on the salt shaker while she grabbed for grains of salt. It is one of the vital minerals in a bird's diet.

Eggshells supply minerals naturally, too. Hens' eggshells, however, could carry Newcastle disease, which is fatal to birds. Bake the eggshells at two hundred degrees or boil them in water for twenty minutes to sterilize them. Oyster shells in bird grit supply the same basic minerals, but eggshells are a favorite with birds. Susie once ate a half eggshell nonstop when she was about to lay her own eggs. Canary breeders feed them to the females before they nest. Eggshells should be crushed before feeding them to birds.

The other vitamins birds need come in special seeds in treat mixtures. Petamine (for finches and canaries) or Budgimine (for budgies, cockies, and lovebirds) are the best treat mixtures. Either product is so safe it may be left in a feed cup in the cage all the time. Other treat mixtures sold in boxes and bottles should be rationed—a half teaspoon (one treat cup) per day. One woman nearly killed her birds with kindness by feeding them treat in their seed dishes and a teaspoon of their basic seed in their treat cups. Fortunately a friend noticed the mistake and told her.

Some seeds in treats have a high fat content. Oats, thistle, and flax, though often needed in the diet, should not be fed to excess. Budgies, for example, should not be given oats and groats as a treat except when they molt, because their basic seed mixture contains all the oats they should have. The fattening seeds should only be fed if a bird has lots of flight room in an aviary, is molting (some species), needs them in the basic diet (some species), is being conditioned to raise young, lives outdoors in winter or in a cold room (under forty-five degrees Fahrenheit or eight degrees centigrade).

Other healthful foods are soybean products, peanut butter, and whole wheat bread. Small amounts of soybean flour are sometimes mixed with the basic seed. Peanut butter is a rich food; the birds in my aviary prefer it fresh. It may take time to teach your bird to eat peanut butter, so be patient. Whole wheat bread may be fed dry or moistened with milk and gently pressed with a fork to remove excess moisture. When wet it spoils and cannot be left long in the cage. Sick birds often relish it when they won't touch anything else. Birds in sunless rooms need a special additive to their diets—cod liver oil or a substitute such as fruits and vegetables which contain vitamin D—to replace natural sunlight.

Birds enjoy treats so much that feeding time turns into one of the best times of the day. Many birds grow tame if you feed them a treat from your hand. My daughter's crimson pileated finch flies to his treat cup to beg whenever she passes the cage. A bird learns to recognize you as the most important person in its life because you hold the key to its treats.

CATCHING AND HOLDING A BIRD

The swift flight of a bird makes you think it would be impossible to catch it if it escaped from its cage. But often a bird will find its way back into the cage without your help. If it must be recaptured, use a bird or fish net, because these can be swung faster than a bird can fly.

An escaped bird—one who has no experience flying loose in the house—should be watched closely. Clever ones dart for cover. Once my husband and I searched for an hour for a baby bird. Finally its mother cocked her eye at a cupboard as if to show us where it had fallen behind the paneling on the wall. We had to remove the panel to rescue it.

Escaped birds are so frightened they often fly into fans, fires, fish tanks, and toilets. Once a red-eared waxbill escaped in my daughter's ninth floor apartment in New York City. She had stuffed rags in the biggest holes between the sashes of the windows, but he found a small one and squirmed to freedom. More birds escape to the wild—and death—through windows than any other way.

An escaped bird must be chased if possible and caught, even though it panics at the sight of a net flying toward it. Try to chase the bird into a small room where it can be cornered easily. The more quickly you catch it, the more merciful you are. A bird feels safest when it can fly to escape, so when you actually hold it in your hand, its fear is intense. Fear drains its energy. Hold an untamed bird for as short a time as possible.

When using a net to catch a bird, hold a thin, light-weight towel in the other hand. Two people make the task easier, because one chases the bird toward the net. As the bird flies, swing the net from behind in the same direction as it flies. If it sees the net coming toward it, it zips around or over the top. As you net the bird, continue the downward loop against the towel so it cannot escape out of the open side of the net. A friend of mine once swung the net against the aviary wall to keep the bird inside it—but the bird's head was outside the net. The frame of the net broke its neck. So use a towel.

The bird, still in the net, may be released by holding the net over the door of the cage. As the bird flies out of the net and into the cage, be sure its toenails do not catch in the netting.

If you cannot catch a bird at all, leave some food and water near its cage and wait until nighttime. Then open the door to the bathroom (or any small room) and turn on the light. Close the toilet. If you turn off all the other lights in the house, the bird will do just what you want—fly to the bathroom. Shut the door and bring out the net. It's easy to catch a bird in a small space.

Nighttime is the easiest time to catch a bird in a small

aviary, too, since birds cannot see in the dark. Flick on a flashlight until you spot it, turn it off quickly, and close your hand gently over the bird. You cannot use this method when birds are nesting, however, because it might frighten the parents off the nests. Leave the lights on after you catch a bird until the other birds settle down.

In large walk-in aviaries, I have found a simple method for catching a bird. Hang a sheet a few feet from one end. Have an assistant hold open the upper corner of the sheet until you chase the bird you want through the opening. When it is confined behind the sheet, it is easy to net.

The first time you catch a bird you may be frightened. "What if I squeeze too hard?" or "What if it bites?" More often the bird cries out so sharply, you let go! A Pekin robin's scream goes right through your head. My black-crested finch keeps on yelling until I release her again.

A bird's beak may frighten you, especially if it is a hook-bill. But a bite isn't dangerous except with parrots. Once I asked a professional bird-bander if he didn't worry about being bitten by the loons he caught. "I let them bite," he said. "When a bird has a hold on your thumb, it focuses on something besides you. Then you can help it." The initial shock of a pinch from a beak startles more than it hurts. It only cuts the skin if you rip your hand away. So take it away gently.

If you still don't want to catch a hook-bill in your hand, drop a washcloth or lightweight towel over it. Wrap it in the folds of the cloth so the material overlaps your fingers where they circle the neck. Then the bird bites cloth, not you. Gloves work poorly because they terrify birds and because you cannot tell if you squeeze too hard.

As you can imagine, it's a joy to own a finger-tamed

bird. Whenever it must be caught, it simply steps on your outstretched finger. Instructions on finger training will be found in the chapter on taming birds.

When catching a bird inside a cage, first take out the perches and swing. Then rest your hand quietly inside the cage until the bird stops fluttering. If it flies about wildly, it may hurt itself. Figure out the spot where it will be easiest to close your hand over it—usually on the floor or against one side. Then *wait*. As soon as the bird lands in that spot, swoop your fingers over it. If you are quick and accurate, the bird won't even flutter.

A bird's body should lie in a natural position, whether it is held through a net, in a towel, or in your bare hand. Its wings should fold flat against its sides; its head should be straight on its neck; its feet should curl up underneath its abdomen or grasp a finger of your hand. Circle its neck with a thumb and forefinger so that just the head peeks out. No matter how small or large a bird is, it must be held gently, because it has hollow bones, which break easily. The lightweight hollow bones enable birds to fly. A sudden squeeze or pressure on a leg or wing can injure it.

Bird-banders have a special method for holding a bird that allows it to flap its wings, thus keeping its body cool. They hold the head between two fingers and the legs between two other fingers, so their hand does not enclose the body. It takes practice to do it gently.

If a bird squirms into an awkward position when you try to hold it, cup it in both hands against your stomach so it has enough room to turn around. It will straighten itself out.

If a bird catches its toes in a net when you are holding it, untangle its nails carefully. Be sure to hold the legs gently as you free it. Think about the *bird*, not the net, as you work so you don't give a careless twist to one leg and break it.

When you want to hand a bird to a friend, let him *take* it. First cup the bird inside your fingers. Then your friend should slide his fingers into yours between your palm and the bird. Your friend will know when he has it securely and can tell you to open your hand. If you try to pass a bird to a friend, the bird often escapes. Just to be safe, always duck into a small room to make the exchange, so you can catch the bird quickly again if it outwits you.

Few things frighten a bird more than being held. It may pant with fear and you may feel its heart pumping. Yet even in fright it recognizes you are trying to help it. A black-crested finch had managed to twist some strands of hair around his leg so tightly, he couldn't free himself. All the time I held him so a girl could cut and unwind the hair, he lay still. But the experience drained his energy so much, he perched without moving for an hour in a corner of the aviary after I let him go. So catch and hold a bird only if you must.

GROOMING

A bird grooms its own feathers. All you supply is the bath. My husband and I fill the baths in the aviary at mealtime each morning so we can watch the entertainment of bathtime. A bird in the bath whirs its feathers so fast, it looks as if it were running an outboard motor. The bath washes away dust, dirt from nesting, and droppings that might have stuck to its feathers. It also helps control mites, a nasty pest. Perhaps the greatest benefit from baths is the ruffled feathers a bird feels impelled to preen afterward. Preening gives feathers a gloss, and without a bath a bird may not preen often enough.

Just as you like tub water the right temperature, so does a bird—only it likes it cooler. Fill its bath with lukewarm water that will cool to room temperature, which is just right. One tame silverbill enjoyed *warm* baths and liked them best when it was cupped in someone's hand with the kitchen faucet trickling onto its back. The water in a birdbath should be the right depth: a half-inch deep for small birds, one inch deep for cockatiels and parrots. If baby chicks might fall in and drown, fill it less than a quarter of an inch for the birds who share their quarters.

Birds who dislike baths should be tempted in every way possible to get wet. My daughter's budgie, Pretty Blue, used to stand near the bath, but never in it. One day when I watered a philodendron nearby, the saucer under the plant overflowed and dripped down the trailing stems. Perhaps it reminded Pretty Blue of a rain forest. It triggered his bathing instinct. He clambered up the plant, wiggling and rubbing against the wet leaves until his feathers were soaked. After that I would always water the philodendron when I wanted him to take a shower.

Birds sometimes will be enticed into a bathtub if a piece of lettuce is floating on the surface of the water. Others, like my blue-winged parrolets, may shove themselves against long, wet lettuce leaves and dampen their feathers. As a last resort a bird's feathers can be moistened with mist from a bottle used to spray plants.

A bird who loves bathing splashes water everywhere. Get everything out of the way, including the seed cups. If you spread a thick towel under the cage, it absorbs the splatters. Large birds may have their birdbaths tucked into the shower or bathtub but don't turn on the faucet! In an aviary the birdbath may be set inside a bird cage so that the plastic guards on the cage will hold spills inside. Also, baby birds won't fall into the tub.

Quail will take baths in grit. They prefer grit that has been stirred until soft and freshly dampened. Reginald and Henrietta, my button quail, twist and roll on their sides into grotesque positions in their efforts to splash sand between their feathers.

As soon as a caged bird completes its bath, remove

the tub. If the tub stays in place, it becomes soiled with droppings and the water will harm a bird who drinks it. Also, a bird bathes more eagerly if its only chance to do so comes when you give it a tub. After a bath—not before—change the paper in the cage.

A bird may be so wet after a bath, it cannot fly. It climbs to a perch and preens itself. Even birds who barely dip their heads in the water will preen. The oil they use for preening comes from a gland under the tail.

The webbed portion of a feather consists of closely spaced barbs. As birds pull each feather through their bills, all the interlocking barbs that make up a feather mesh neatly to form a smooth flight surface. The ruffled look vanishes. Ornithologists say to beware of attributing human feelings to birds, but after a bath a bird does seem to look happy.

Let birds bathe in the morning, if possible, so all their feathers can dry before dark. Feathers dry slowly and birds will feel cold if they are still wet when going to sleep.

A wet bird is susceptible to drafts. You may need to cover a portion of the cage until the bird dries. A sick bird won't take a bath—a warning signal to its owner.

Fountains make pretty additions to areas where birds live. In our garden room my husband and I had a fish-shaped fountain that shot water from its mouth. The birds kept their distance. They seem to prefer shallow pools of water or a stream trickling from a hose. A fancy fountain may cost a thousand dollars, but inexpensive plastic ones may be found for less than a hundred. The aviary must be large to contain a fountain or it creates too much humidity. High humidity causes a "soft," or out-of-season, molt and can cause feathers to break off. In large rooms—like the aviaries at zoos—the high humidity does not harm birds because of the abundant sunshine there and the high upper areas for flight. A small room confines the humidity and it masks everything.

Whether your bird bathes by a fountain, a pool, or a tub, the grooming that follows is good for its feathers. Birds cannot do all grooming tasks for themselves. In the wild, rough bark and rocks trim their nails. In a cage, however, a bird lands and takes off less frequently than it would outside, so its nails may become overgrown. Then their feet get sore.

Long toenails curve into a half circle. Sometimes they jut out sideways so they look deformed. When you buy your bird, its toenails should not meet underneath the perch. If you suddenly notice the toes forming a closed circle around the perch, they are too long. If a bird clings to the perch with its foot as it takes off, causing its body to jerk a bit, the nails are getting long. If it catches its nail on something so it hangs by its leg for a moment, the nails are too long and should be cut at once.

There's nothing wrong with a bird whose toenails grow long. The nails just grow on some birds, while never needing a trim on others. The birds most likely to have overgrown toenails are strawberry finches, spice finches, nuns, and pintailed nonpareils. Even canaries need their nails trimmed four times a year. Let a vet or someone experienced with birds show you how to trim toenails before attempting it.

When you feel confident enough to cut toenails, hold the bird in one hand with its legs secure between two fingers. Use bird clippers—sold by suppliers—or toenail clippers made for dogs, which have a hole into which the nail fits to be cut. Birds often grip the hole, making the task easy. A nail may be filed also—the safest way for a beginner to do it. Hold the foot steady as you file.

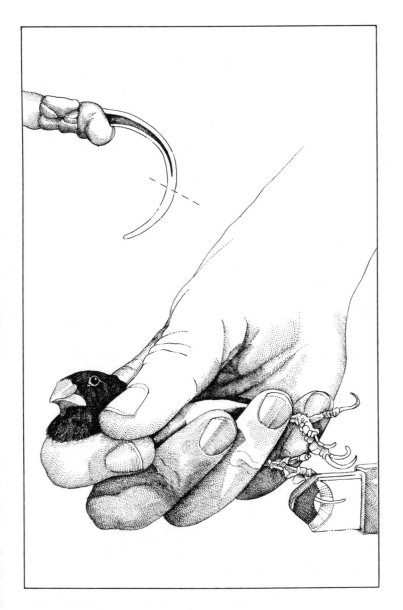

Long toenails curve in a half circle. Clip to within an eighth or a fourth of an inch from the vein.

A strong light or magnifying glass will help you see a vein running down the middle of the nail. It looks like a thin, red line. In dark-colored nails it is more difficult to see. Trim the nail almost to the vein—with an eighth to a quarter of an inch to spare. Cut a little at a time. After you have done it many times, you will be able to cut it to the correct length in one snip. Take care the bird's foot isn't twisted as you work.

The nail will bleed if you cut the vein, but the bleeding can be stopped with a styptic pencil or by pressing flour or cornstarch tightly onto the nail. A paper towel soaked in cold water and held tightly against the toe also stanches the bleeding. A bird should be watched for several hours afterward in case the bleeding should start again.

A bird's bill sometimes grows too long, or the upper mandible—the top half of the bill—crosses over the lower one. A vet should trim the bill for you. With many birds it won't happen again, but some have bills that grow like Pinocchio's nose. A vet can show you how to cut off the tip with dog's toenail clippers so it meets evenly again. Sometimes a bird who sits on eggs won't take time to trim its bill, so it grows a pointed tip. However, once the young hatch, it will break off the long tip on the cuttlebone, so don't rush to give it aid until you are sure it needs it.

As hook-bills grow up, they break little pieces off their bills, causing the edges to look irregular. This is their method for trimming their own bills. A neat, perfectly formed bill is undesirable in an adult hook-bill. The bill should not touch the chest either. A vet will trim or file an overgrown bill. It's a tricky task, because the vein grows out with the beak. Also, unless it is cut off in diagonal pieces, it may split up the middle or crack. The way to prevent overgrown beaks is to give your hook-bill chewable toys—rawhide sticks made for puppies, plastic toys, a piece of knotted rope, mineral blocks and salt spools, and hardwood tree limbs. These toys also help prevent boredom.

A special kind of grooming—clipping the wings—will be needed to tame a bird. Then it cannot escape while you work with it. If their wings are clipped, aggressive birds in an aviary cannot chase their enemies. A friend of mine hates birds because a budgie she took care of as a child used to escape from its cage and attack her whenever she came in the room. If the bird's wings had been clipped, it might have tormented her less.

Generally when the wings are clipped, the long flight feathers—the primaries—are cut. This doesn't hurt a bird, for it has no sensation in its feathers. No more than half a feather should be trimmed, however, or it will bleed and hurt. Before clipping, gently spread out the wing feathers like a fan. Draw an imaginary line parallel to the bird's body that runs from the shorter feathers—the secondaries—to the top of the wing. The line should go through the primaries about a third of the way down from the tips. On a budgie or cockie this includes six to eight feathers. If the two outermost feathers are left unclipped, the beauty of the wing line is preserved.

Only one wing needs to be clipped for taming a hook-bill because then it is off balance and flies in circles. This discourages flying! Finches need both wings clipped and sometimes the tips of the secondaries or they fly too well to be tamed. An aggressive bird needs both wings clipped to impair its flying ability. A bird must be able to fly a little or it cannot break a fall with its wings—and it may be hurt.

The feathers will be replaced with new, long ones

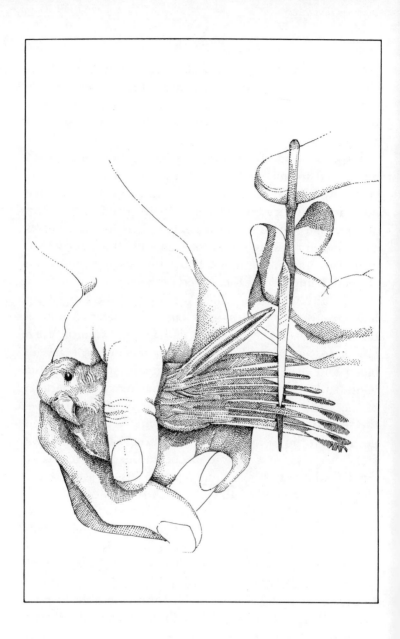

When clipping a wing, clip no more than half of each feather.

during the bird's first molt and it will be able to fly perfectly again. By then a tame bird no longer wants to fly away from its owner. Parrots, in fact, seldom fly again, as if they had forgotten how. But don't take a chance on your pet's not remembering its days of flight and take it outdoors—you may lose it. Aggressive birds must be clipped again and again, because their character won't change.

Don't let anyone convince you a bird should be pinioned—have its upper wing joint removed to prevent it from flying. This is a cruel and painful thing to do. If the wings are clipped properly, a bird cannot escape.

A bird's life depends on correct grooming. It may dislike having it done, because it dislikes being handled. But afterward it will ruffle its feathers, stretch its wings, and forget all about it.

10

TRAVELING WITH A BIRD

In all the excitement of a trip, plans have to be made for your bird. Should it stay home with a bird-sitter or travel with the family or be boarded in a pet store or with a vet? When you are moving to another city, you *know* it goes with you. Your bird will arrive safely if you pack as carefully for it as you do for yourself.

A bird will travel more comfortably in its own cage than in anything else. If the car is cramped for space, it can travel in a carrying cage, a smaller than normal cage, for a trip of a day or two.

The cage should be escape-proof. Twist pipe cleaners around the joints if the roof is removable. Tape the tray securely so it cannot fall out if the cage tips over. A pipe cleaner may act as a lock on the cage door, or a real lock may be used if the bird is clever at opening things. Anything loose, such as a toy or dish, could hit the bird if the car stopped suddenly, so tape or wire everything in place. Be sure the bird cannot catch its toenail in any fastening you use. The perches you normally keep in the cage will give your bird its best grip while the car is moving. A bird's foot is designed to hold something roundish, and the grip automatically tightens when it sleeps. If forced to sit on the cage floor, a bird slips and slides around with every jarring motion.

When traveling you cannot depend on finding pet stores that sell the right seed, so always take enough from home. Also take water in a tightly closed jar. On a long trip you will have to buy bottled water to be sure it is fresh and clean and has nothing added to it that will upset your bird's digestion.

Seed should be spread on the floor of the cage to make it easy to eat, but fill a cup with it, too. An automatic bottle feeder with a ball bearing nozzle may be used on smooth roads without leaking much. Otherwise give your bird a drink whenever you stop—at least three or four times a day. And let it eat and drink for an hour or more before covering it at night.

Do not introduce all the new dishes and water containers on the day of the trip, when a bird will face new experiences and confusion. While your bird is still comfortably at home, put it in the new cage with everything there you plan to use while traveling.

Drafts, killers at home, have the same power in a car. An open window may pour a delightful breeze into the car for the riders, but a bird won't enjoy it. In hot weather all it needs is a sheet wrapped around its cage for protection. When it is cold outdoors, wrap the cage in a bath towel, but be sure the car is warm before bringing your bird into it each day. Don't set the cage near the heater; you might roast your bird.

When my family traveled from Connecticut to Florida one winter, our daughter had just started taming a zebra finch, Poof. If she left the bird behind, she would have to give up training it; so we took it along. Poof made the trip in style, even finding a place in motels that barred other pets. Though the weather changed from freezing to summer warmth, with care Poof never suffered a day of discomfort. He became the tamest of finches by journey's end.

If a bird is to fly on a plane with you, check the airlines about the size requirements for the shipping box and make a reservation to keep the bird in the cabin with you. Some airlines no longer require reservations for birds; others refuse to take them except in a special luggage compartment designed for animals. The restrictions on international travel are so complex you should begin conquering the obstacles at least six months before traveling abroad or returning to this country with a bird.

A traveling cage or a shipping box designed for birds must fit under an airplane seat. It should have a perch fastened securely inside, and all the other precautions mentioned for car travel should be taken. If you use a cage, set it inside a ventilated cardboard box to protect the bird from drafts. The box will need a window; otherwise a bird cannot see to eat while it is traveling.

A bird causes all sorts of problems when you are traveling, so don't be tempted to buy one while vacationing. It is so easy to be swayed into choosing a bird that way, and you cannot return it. It is hard on a bird to be carried about for days on end with strangers in a car. Many a family who would have enjoyed a bird in their own home has come to dislike the idea after being confined with the bird while traveling.

By far the easiest way to travel is without your bird. A seedeating bird may be left at home safely for two or three days. Leave a cereal bowl (or aluminum pie tin) of seed on the cage floor, hang some spray millet about the cage, and add enough extra water containers to hold an abundant supply. A bottle with a nozzle—if your bird has learned to drink from one—keeps the water fresh and clean. If possible, find someone to check on the bird each day.

A bird may be boarded with a vet or at a pet shop. The one you choose depends on the people who will take care of your bird. Once, at a vet's, I noticed a cage of lovebirds on the front desk. They had become the mascots of the assistants and couldn't have had better care. But I also know a woman in the pet department in the basement of a discount store who has more knowledge of birds than anyone in the town and gives her boarders exceptional care. So pick the pet shop as carefully as if you were buying a bird there, or find a vet who knows birds and whom you can trust.

For long vacations you may prefer a wise and loving bird-sitter. Leave an emergency number for a vet or breeder who will answer questions the sitter might have. Write out—don't just explain—how to care for your bird. Include instructions on diet, cleaning, filling water containers (and how to keep the correct sections of tube feeders together), what to do if the bird escapes in the house, and the importance of companionship. I have my bird-sitters go through a three-day trial period. Even so, it is difficult to think of all the emergencies. Once a bird-sitter couldn't open the lock on our door. It took the neighbors, the police, and a locksmith to get her into the house.

Psittacines need more than food and water when you are away. They must have human companionship and attention. If a hook-bill is left with a friend, the friend must be one who loves birds and wants one for company. Even finches and canaries become lonely if left alone for more than a day or two. A tamed finch or canary needs companionship just as a psittacine does.

Whenever you leave your bird behind, it will come to know the person who cares for it just as it knows you. But it will still give you a joyous welcome when you return home.

11

TAMING AND
TRAINING A BIRD

A tame bird sits on its owner's hand and peeps or whistles at him. A bird bought the day it learns to eat for itself and no longer needs its parents to feed it can usually be tamed, because it has not yet developed a fear of humans. Only tame birds learn to talk.

A bird must be isolated from all other birds to become tame. It must have its wings clipped, too. (See grooming chapter.) The first few days you bring it home are the critical ones, because the older it grows, the harder it will be to tame. So plan to spend a lot of time with a bird at the beginning.

The ways to obtain a bird that is young enough to tame are to buy it from a breeder, or a pet shop where birds are raised, or to raise it yourself. (See the next chapter.) Sometimes a pet store sells birds young enough to tame because the owners finger-tame the birds or buy from a local breeder. Not all birds can be tamed even if they are young, so the right species determines your choice. The common ones are zebra finches, budgies and cockatiels. Try to find a budgie close to six weeks old, a zebra finch between nine and twelve days after it left the nest, or a cockie that has had some training as a nestling.

Zebra finches' beaks turn from black to orange as they mature. By the time the beak is half orange, when the bird is about three and a half weeks old, it is too late to tame it. This method of telling age does not work with white zebras because their bills start out pink. You will have to trust the person who sells such a finch to tell you its correct age. This is also true of society finches because neither their bills nor plumage changes color during the first month when they are young enough to tame.

Immature budgies have black, wavy lines on their foreheads just above their bills. These lines disappear as the budgie matures. If you buy one while it still has these lines, it will be much easier to tame than an older bird. A cockatiel that is under six months of age can be tamed, although the younger it is the easier it will be. Many pet shops and breeders spend the time to hand-tame cockatiels. Such birds make by far the best pets.

Most people prefer males. Among finches, the males sing. With budgies and cockies, the males have the potential to learn more words when they are trained to talk. Telling the sexes of such young birds, however, is tricky. Male zebra finches sing a raspy song when they are only three or four weeks old, but you have to be around when they are practicing, and they do not try to sing often. Gray zebra males often have tiny black tips to one or two breast feathers. Only an expert can guess with budgies, although I have a friend who raises them and says the females bite harder. A person who is skilled with cockies can sometimes detect a few bright yellow feathers on the face of males when they are about five months old.

An immature budgie (*bottom*)—with dark bars on its forehead—is easier to tame than an adult (*top*).

However, the advantages of males are highly overrated. Female finches make loyal and adoring pets. Female budgies I have trained were easier to tame and became gentler pets than males. Many female budgies have been taught to speak as many phrases as males tamed by the same person. Both sexes of cockatiels learn to talk.

The kind of pet you have after training depends almost entirely upon you. The quieter you are, the more patience you have, the more time you spend playing with your bird, the tamer a pet you will have. Unfortunately, no one can guarantee a budgie or cockie will learn to mimic sounds—to talk. A few seem unable to learn. They will still be tame and entertaining pets even without a vocabulary. Be sure, when you buy a bird, the seller clips one or both wings so you will have an easier time taming it.

Taming a bird means winning its confidence and affection so it sits on your hand or arm. If you frighten it, it will never trust you. A bird is frightened by a hand closing over it, by being held so it cannot fly, and by a trainer who makes sudden movements, talks loudly, or is rough when touching it.

A small room like a bathroom makes the best training area. The lid on the toilet should be closed and the faucets off if you use a bathroom. Let the bird out of its cage. If it won't fly out, remove the bottom of the cage and all the perches.

The bird will fly a short distance even with its wings clipped. It will land on a curtain rod, its cage, or the floor. To tame it, slide your open hand underneath it. *Never close your fingers around a bird.* It has no reason to fear your hand; in fact it makes a warm, nestlike cup or a firm, round, finger-size perch. Cockatiels prefer the broad edge of your hand. A bird exercises by flying and will continue to fly even after it is tame, so don't be dismayed when it leaves your hand to fly again. Simply slip your hand underneath it when it lands. Do it over and over again until it sees that no matter where it goes, it will end up on your hand anyway.

When it is sitting on your hand, swing it gently back and forth and up and down. Encourage it to step onto the finger of your other hand by pressing your finger against its chest in front of its legs and gently pushing backward. It must either step up or fall over. After stepping up with one foot it may give you a surprised look as it finds its foot moving. A hook-bill will test the finger with its bill to see if it is steady enough to step on—it is not trying to bite. Keep your finger motionless and firm, and it will step up. Make a ladder for it to walk up—a finger from one hand, a finger from the other, and so on. Slip the bird onto your shoulder or arm in the same way.

The training periods should run a half hour to an hour three or four times a day the first few days. When the bird sits willingly on your hand and shoulder, the battle for taming is won. When it flies to you, it trusts and likes you. Avoid letting a bird sit on your head during the training period—lift it off onto your hand—because it does not associate your head with you as it does your shoulder or hand. Not only will the bird be less tame, it is difficult to lift droppings off your hair.

Older birds will need more lessons, and your patience may be tried to the limit. Sometimes older birds who cannot be tamed to your hand can be perch-tamed. Parrots, who will bite a hand in taming (and who are terrified of gloves), may be perch-tamed with a long period of training and much kindness. Use a perch similar to one in the bird's cage. Have both of the bird's wings clipped to limit flying as much as possible. Hold the perch in front of the bird, then move it against its chest until it steps on it. Move the perch up and down gently, talk constantly to the bird, and bring it close to your body so it knows you. After a week or so you may be able to persuade it to step onto your arm from the perch. This will give you a feeling of real accomplishment.

Flighty birds may also be difficult to tame. Sometimes they panic because their nature is flighty, sometimes because they are old enough to fear humans. Such a bird needs to adjust to the sight of you close to its cage until it ceases to flutter when you are there. Keep its cage nearby whenever possible—while watching TV, studying, or reading. Next rest your hand motionless inside the cage. When it accepts your hand, try moving a finger against its chest while it sits on a perch. Tidbits of food may encourage it to step onto your finger. When it will sit on your hand, training continues in the same pattern as for any bird. A twelve-year-old boy trained an adult silverbill, but it took months. Eventually it flew to his shoulder whenever it saw him and slept in his hand. So don't despair in training a bird; keep trying, and you may succeed against all odds.

The greatest aids in taming are a gentle way of handling a bird and a light, kind voice. A bird won't care what you say, but will enjoy the tone, even a cheep, or a whistle.

Birds quickly discover the joy of freedom and dislike returning to their cages. A tame bird may ride back into its cage on your finger, the best way of returning it. However, if it flies off when it nears the doorway, a treat inside may lure it to return. It can always be fed *after* training sessions. A few of its favorite seeds may be sprinkled on the floor of the room, and while it eats them, the cage with its bottom removed, may be set over it. At night a bird may be tricked into its cage by turning out the light as it rides on your finger toward the cage. Move your hand inside, cover the door with your body, and turn on the light. Most tame birds eventually return to their cages by themselves so they can eat.

If a bird grows too independent with its freedom and refuses to come to you, it may need retraining. Take it into the bathroom again and repeat its early lessons.

You've taken on an important responsibility when you've tamed a bird. It is no longer content to be by itself but needs human company. One pet store owner has learned that he must spend time with his hook-bill at home each night no matter how late it may be. Otherwise the bird feels so thwarted, it calls to him and keeps him awake all night. A neglected bird may turn nasty and begin attacking people who visit the house.

Birds other than budgies, cockatiels, and zebra and society finches can be tamed. Green singing finches, canaries, and doves make tame pets if bought when young enough. The button quail, a comical bird, will waddle and scramble after its owner, but only those raised in incubators become tame. Quail have feathers that fall out if you pick them up, however. Wild starlings, if taken from the nest and hand-fed, will also become tame. A parrot tamed by the breeder when still a nestling makes an unusually tame pet. Some young parrots are coming on the market now that have had training by the trappers who take them from the nest. They will sit on your hand in the pet store when you buy them. There are also many instances of an owner working for months to win an adult parrot's trust so it becomes a pal. Some species of parrots, however, can never be tamed.

Once a bird is tame, talking lessons can begin. Taming helps a bird learn to talk because it pays attention to its owner and responds to him. It listens for its owner's voice.

A bird mimics sounds without understanding what they mean. After it hears a sound often enough, it may repeat it. Hook-bills delight in whistling, and if they learn to whistle first, they often refuse to talk.

Begin teaching a bird to talk during the day when it is content and happy or it won't learn. Hold it close to your mouth so it sees you form the sounds.

Decide on a simple word with one or two distinct sounds. Birds seem to like the sound of "pretty," but "hi there," "hello," or the bird's name may be used instead. The first word takes the longest to teach. Stick to that one word. Say it over and over again. Keep up the lesson for an hour, boring as it may be to you, and repeat the lesson every day. Say the word whenever you come into the room, when you change the cage or feed your bird.

Birds find it easier to mimic high pitched voices. Listen carefully because a bird may mimic the word with such terrible pronunciation or with such birdlike tones or so unclearly, you fail to recognize it. Its pronunciation will improve. Months may pass before a bird suddenly says the word—or it may take only a couple of weeks.

The second word comes more easily to a bird. Stick to the new word until it is learned, then add a third. If you use a training record, find one that repeats only one word. You will need to learn to say the word exactly as it is repeated on the record for the bird to recognize it when you say it. Once it learns its first word from a record, it is better if you teach it any additional words. It may learn only one word, or it may learn a hundred—a few birds have.

A bird cannot answer a question since it cannot understand speech. It may *seem* to answer a question. If it learns the words, "What is your name? Pretty Blue," when someone asks, "What is your name?" it will complete the phrase with "Pretty Blue."

An untamed bird that has talking ability might learn to talk if you are patient enough. A friend of mine had an African gray parrot, one of the birds with the highest potential for talking in the world. Every morning when she went into its room, she said, "Good morning, Billy." Silence. Billy would not talk. But she repeated the phrase every morning. One day eighteen months later as she opened the door, her parrot said, "Good morning, Billy." After that it added one phrase after another to its vocabulary.

A bird cannot unlearn a word. A mynah left at a pet store during vacation picked up a nasty word from a man it disliked in the store. As soon as the bird returned home and a visitor it disliked arrived, the mynah repeated the word. The owner blushed. Forever afterward, she feared hearing that word in the mynah's mouth. Some words sound funny at first. Gabby and Sam, two yellow-napped Amazons, used to sing "Row, Row, Row Your Boat" for children at a zoo. But the birds liked the song so much and sang it so often, the children soon covered their ears and cried, "No, not again." Be sure a word a bird learns will bear repeating a thousand times.

One yellow-fronted Amazon sings trills, scales, and ornaments from French operas and has a range of six octaves. Beautiful melodies remain beautiful no matter how often they are sung by a bird.

It would be difficult to grow tired of a canary's song, it is so musical and varied. My daughter's canary once lost its song by mimicking a green singing finch. A canary breeder told her to play a canary recording for her bird when it finished molting. That is the time of year when

canaries that compete in singing contests go through
retraining. My daughter's canary relearned its repertoire,
too. Your canary will pick up new variations to its song
if you play a record of canary songs in the fall after it
molts.

Surprisingly some birds have been housebroken—a
different kind of training. A hook-bill sometimes can be
taught to eliminate in its cage. It is taught by associating
the act with a word. Pick a simple word that won't em-
barrass you if the bird repeats it. I use "hurry up" for my
dog, and it can be used for a bird as well, but any word,
even one not in the English language, will do. Repeat
the word whenever the bird leaves a dropping on your
shoulder or in its cage. After a few weeks it will associate the word with its squatting act. Try repeating the
word just before taking the bird from its cage. Praise it
if it leaves a dropping. Never scold for mistakes—that's
beyond its ability to understand. A bird needs to leave a
dropping every twenty minutes or so; it must be returned
to its cage, and the word repeated, if you don't want
spots around.

Some trainers have a knack for teaching birds to do
tricks. Merwin, a budgie, scoots into his mistress's pocket
and rides around there. Some parrots learn to push tiny
carts and do somersaults. Hook-bills entertain themselves
by swinging upside down and may do it on a perch you
hold in your hand. A bird often climbs a ladder when a
treat lies enticingly at the top.

Once you have worked hard to train a bird, don't take
chances with it. No matter how tame it seems, don't
tempt it to leave you by taking it outdoors on a fine
summer day. A sudden fright might make it leave your
shoulder, and once lost, a bird seldom finds home again.
Peter, a budgerigar in England, flew out an open window.

Somehow he escaped the cats and birds of prey for eleven days. Then a man found him and nursed him back to health. Suddenly Peter talked in numbers. When the man dialed the numbers on the phone, Peter's delighted owner answered. But few lost bird stories have such a happy ending.

12

BREEDING

The tiny peeps of baby chicks in the nest always rouse a feeling of wonder at the workings of nature. You may have many reasons for raising birds, from a biology project at school to a curiosity about birds' habits. It may be a hobby or a means to earn money. Perhaps before you realize it, you will be making a contribution to ecology. The people who bred Bourke's parakeet in England and the United States could hardly have dreamed the offspring would be flown to Australia to reintroduce the species there when it was threatened with extinction.

Zebra finches, since they are probably the easiest species for the amateur to breed, can be used as a model of how to raise birds. These finches come in many colors, but gray zebra finches will be easiest for the beginner to breed. Many species of birds—like zebra finches—come in a multitude of colors, some of which predominate among the genes no matter how many genes are present. These dominant colors reproduce more easily than the recessive—less dominant—ones.

As a beginner it is wise to start with birds who are not related. Many breeders who are anxious to develop a special color or strain of birds will interbreed to achieve their goal. However, breeders choose the finest examples and healthiest birds they own. They also recognize and avoid genetic defects. As a basic guide, do not mate brothers and sisters. Such combinations in the hands of an amateur can accentuate defects and even produce deformed offspring. When you start to breed, the parents should be the healthiest birds you can find.

Since zebra finch cocks (the males) and hens (the females) have different markings, even an amateur can pick one bird of each sex. Only with white or pied zebra finches is it difficult to distinguish the sexes. If the birds are adults, however, you can usually tell the cocks because their bills are brighter red than the hens' bills. With gray zebra finches the cocks have colorful markings on their cheeks, chests, and sides which hens lack. The cocks always sing, too, and the hens lay eggs.

It's better not to mate a pet bird, especially a tame one. The bird may become happier with its mate than with its owner, and you lose a friendly companion. Some pet birds make poor parents. Your bird may be too old to breed, too.

Two pairs of birds sharing an aviary are more likely to breed than a single pair. Most birds have a colony instinct and trigger one another to action from something as simple as bathing together to something as complex as nesting. The birds you buy as parents—your stock— may all be loosed at the same time in a large flight cage or an aviary where they will quickly pair off. Two pairs in the same territory prevent all sorts of problems from developing. One pair of birds nesting in a cage, for example, chase each other, because of an urge to defend the nest from *someone*.

The birds not only like the extra room in an aviary, but need it to exercise. Hens have less trouble with egg-binding (trouble laying an egg) if they have lots of exercise.

Unlike most species zebra finches will nest at any time of year. Other species wait for the right season—spring. Sometimes they can be triggered into nesting with a longer day of twelve to fifteen hours created by fluorescent lights or with temperatures of sixty-five to seventy F (eighteen to twenty-one C). Zebra finches like to nest so much one man raised his in temperatures twelve degrees below zero F (twenty-four below C)—but this is hardly normal and would take a period of adjustment for the parents. Many species need insects, seeding grasses, and special foods to nest, but zebra finches are easier to please. They *can* eat their normal diet right up to the time the young hatch, but extra foods, especially mealworms, help condition them. Conditioning is simply adding rich foods to a bird's diet to strengthen it and encourage it to breed. Hens appreciate extra eggshells to eat before nesting because the calcium helps them to produce their own eggs.

Zebra finches decide on their own when to raise young, but they cannot reproduce until they are mature. This happens early with zebra finches, sometimes at three months, but it could be as late as nine months old. Hens should be eight or nine months old before mating. If they are too young, they may have trouble with egg-binding. Cocks may be a bit younger than hens. Breeders often mate an experienced bird with a young one so the older bird trains the younger one. Neither bird in a pair should be molting when it starts nesting. It puts too much of a strain on a bird to molt *and* raise young at the same time.

Birds need a container to hold the nest they build. The crotch of a tree or thick clusters of leaves they could use in the wild do not exist in a cage. Zebra finches build inside nesting boxes, square plywood boxes with a hole near the top on one side. Some will nest in wicker baskets, and a few will build a nest from scratch among artificial or real greenery. They have been known to nest in tumbleweed if it is picked when dry and brown, shaken free of spiders, and washed and dried. Even a pile of hay in a mesh container may intrigue them, though it is more likely they will empty the container, carrying the hay elsewhere for a nest.

Nests can be built of many types of material, beginning with the coarser ones such as thin twigs and hay or even grass from the field—if it is washed and dried first. Salt marsh hay works especially well because it does not absorb moisture from the babies' excrement. Nesting hair can be bought from suppliers and if washed and sterilized after the nest is deserted, can be reused. Burlap, however, makes the most popular material. It should be cut into pieces an inch to two inches square and unraveled. A few pieces may be threaded onto a wire and hung in the aviary; then the birds unravel it themselves and seem proud of each piece they wrest from the pile. It is easier to unravel a loosely woven type of burlap. Choose a natural-colored type rather than one that has been dyed, for the color comes off on the birds. Burlap should be boiled or laundered before making it into a nesting material.

Zebra finches could win the championship for nest building. In fact they are so enthusiastic, they will build one nest on top of another, each one complete with un-hatched eggs. They can only build as high as the roof of the box, however, so you can prevent sandwiching by filling the box half-full of hay before giving it to the birds. As soon as the nest takes form, you can give them smaller amounts of nesting material each day or make it harder to pull out the material. This is a good time to let them unravel their own squares of burlap.

The wrong kind of nesting material can tangle in a bird's toes or around its legs. A bird pecks at it, tightening it. If it isn't removed, the bird may lose its toes or its foot. The young snag their feet, too. Avoid using dog hair, string, thread, cotton, or wool. Boxes of nesting *material*, rather than nesting *hair*, may contain string. I have had this material, short as it is, twist about a bird's leg. Human hair, pulled off while you work around the aviary, can also be picked up by birds and catch on their toes.

The zebra finch cock builds the nest, but the hen does some of the weaving of the offerings he brings. She'll lay her eggs when the nest has been lined with something soft. Sometimes she carries feathers to the nest herself for the lining.

Birds dislike humans peeking inside their nests, though zebras mind less than most birds. If your curiosity drives you to look inside, choose a time when both birds are off the nest eating. They can be away from the nest for twenty minutes or so at a time; they seem to know how long the eggs stay warm without them. Don't touch the nest, however, because even one piece of hay pushed awry may make them desert the eggs. With all other breeding birds the most important rule is: Never disturb them by peeking into the nest, moving something near-by, or touching the nest.

About two weeks after the hen lays, the young hatch. However, the incubation period varies, and it's quite difficult for an amateur to count the days. So allow three weeks from the time you think the eggs were laid before you start to despair about their hatching. Birds have a brood patch on their chests—a place where the feathers will part to allow them to warm the eggs. Even though they sit in the nest, they may not start brooding immediately. The warmth of the room also affects how fast the eggs hatch. Since the eggs are laid on different days, they won't all hatch on the same day. The cock and the hen take turns sitting on the eggs.

There are many signs the young have hatched, and if you learn them, you won't have to peek in the nest during the first critical days after hatching. The hen often gathers feathers to make the nest softer for the young. You might hear the faintest whispering sound after the parents return to the nest—it is the babies asking to be fed. You have to listen from a place where the parents cannot see you because they hush the young if they fear someone will hear them. When the young are so small, spend as little time working in the aviary as possible so the parents can feed them without interruption. If they are bothered too much, they may sit too close on the young and can even kill a baby—though zebra finches are less guilty of this than other species.

Zebra finches have the ability to raise young on seed alone, but the results are better if you help out with a special supply of foods that are easy to digest. Scrambled eggs are one of the easiest foods to give. Supply fresh ones four times a day. Mealworms, too, if the zebras will eat them, make a high protein food for the young. Nestling food, a special mixture consisting mostly of bread crumbs or a cereal base such as ground cornflakes, can be bought commercially, or you may make your own. A dish of this food can be left for the birds to find. Breeders mix it with egg, but since it spoils quickly when wet, it is better for a beginner to leave the mixing to the birds. Many birds like corn at this time because they can make it into a soft, curdlike food called milk crop. These extra foods should be given to the birds twelve days after the eggs are laid or left in the cage each day during the nesting period just to be sure they are there when the young hatch. When these foods start to disappear rapidly, you know the birds have young to feed.

The zebra finch cock shares in feeding the young. The parents eat food themselves, then regurgitate it into the babies' mouths. The young grow quickly, so supply plenty of food every day.

Two weeks after they hatch zebra young will have feathers all over their bodies and be almost as large as their parents. This is when they emerge from the nest and fly—or fledge—for the first time. The day before they fledge, you'll catch sight of a baby in the doorway of its nest with its head peering over the edge or stretching its wings as if it were trying to gather enough courage to leave. The first day the fledglings (the young) emerge, the parents flutter over them constantly, call them from perch to perch, feed them, and finally steer them back to the nest again.

The parents continue feeding their young for another couple of weeks after they fledge. The cock will feed them longer than the hen will. As soon as she feels the fledglings should be weaned, she will peck them away from her. The young peep especially loudly when they are being weaned because the parents refuse to feed them enough in order to make them begin eating for themselves. The last baby that fledged will be the last

Zebra finches and their young

one weaned, though how the parents know is a mystery only they can answer. If two broods hatch at the same time, each set of parents recognizes and feeds its own offspring, though all the fledglings may look identical to you. I had a female strawberry finch, though, who would feed any baby in the aviary who begged for food. The baby zebra finches would follow her around. Occasionally zebra finches help feed each other's offspring, too.

If you plan to tame a baby zebra finch from one clutch —a nestful—it can be marked. Use food coloring (which isn't poisonous) so you can tell the baby apart from its brothers and sisters. Watch closely after the sixth day from fledging on to see how soon it cracks seed and eats for itself. It should eat a lot at a time and do so frequently to be truly self-feeding. This will be sometime between the sixth and twelfth day after fledging. If you aren't sure, wait an extra day, because it will die if taken too soon from its parents. The younger it is, the more quickly it will become tame.

If you plan to sell or give away the young, wait until they are at least five or six weeks old. Age is counted, when selling them, from the day they are born.

Zebra finches will renest as soon as the young are weaned. Breeders are careful not to let them have more than three broods a year in case overbreeding should result in weak young or weakened parents. If the number of nests is restricted, the birds raise more young in each brood; a single baby to a clutch is not unusual with zebra finches who nest continuously. You can prevent birds from renesting if you remove the nesting boxes and nesting material or if you separate the sexes.

Other species of birds have slightly different requirements to breed successfully, but if you learn to breed zebra finches, you will then be able to cope with the added difficulties of other kinds of birds. Among the hook-bills, budgies breed the most easily. They, too, nest more willingly if there are two or more pairs together. Budgies, in fact, usually refuse to nest if they are the only pair doing it. The nesting box needs to be deeper and larger than for zebra finches and has a hollowed out place on the floor to hold the eggs together. You probably won't need any nesting material. Most budgies throw it out of the nest, although one woman told me her budgies constructed a neat, round nest for their eggs.

Canaries are difficult birds to breed, because they demand strict attention to time tables and detail. An amateur should start with colony breeding because it is easier and more likely to work. The open nests canaries like have become known as "canary nests." It can be as simple as a small strainer used in the kitchen and lined with a piece of felt. Breeding season coincides with our spring, but conditioning begins by the end of January with the addition of special foods to the diet.

Some of the birds easy to raise include doves, society finches, and button quail. You might have success with cut-throat finches, but they refuse to breed for some people no matter how the birds are coddled. Button quail should be the offspring of natural parents in order to breed. Those raised in incubators don't seem to understand about sitting on a nest.

Many little problems arise when you try to breed birds. You might be shocked one day to find a baby bird wiggling on the floor of the aviary. Pick it up carefully and set it back in the nest. Sometimes a bit of nest repairing is in order then. By tipping the nest or taping a small extension on one side or adding a bit of extra nesting material in the right place, you might make it more difficult for the baby to squirm out a second time. Don't alter the inside of the nest. If the baby seems dead, try cupping it in your hands and blowing warm air over it—it might revive.

Occasionally a baby dies in the nest. If you should discover a dead baby, remove it. The rest of the nestlings will probably be all right.

In an emergency it might be necessary to feed a nestling. It will need some warm, damp food. A mixture of scrambled eggs that have been pressed through a sieve and bread crumbs or nestling food should be moistened with warm water. The food may be picked up on the tip of a toothpick or with tweezers. It goes *over* the chick's tongue; otherwise it won't go down its throat. Take care not to poke it with the toothpick or to let food dribble into the nostrils at the top of the beak, because it could choke to death.

If a chick won't open its mouth, rub a bit of food on the bill. When it opens its beak to clean off the food, pop in a mouthful. Chicks open their mouths when turned upside down, too, or if you wiggle your fingers as if they were wings flying toward it—the way a chick sees its parents coming with food.

After the incubation period has passed, if none of the eggs hatch, the fault could be yours because you disturbed the bird too much or caused it to fly off its nest and stay away so long the eggs grew cold. It might also be the bird's fault. Inexperienced birds make mistakes; but a second chance may help them correct the error.

Possibly the eggs were infertile. They can be "candled," a word that originated with the use of candlelight to examine eggs. Take a small box and cut a tiny hole in the top that is slightly smaller than the bird's eggs. Set a flashlight inside so the beam shines through the hole. Then when the egg is placed over the hole, the light shines through it. If the egg is fertile, not only should the yolk be seen floating in the white, but a dark spot that is the embryo of the chick should be there, too. Sometimes you can see veins in the developing egg. If you discover the eggs *are* fertile, put them back in the nest again for the hen to hatch.

When birds finish nesting, everything should be cleaned to spotless beauty—the nests, the aviary, the area around the aviary. Cleanliness is one of the keys to raising young birds successfully.

Once the young are weaned, they can be moved to a different cage from their parents. Parents who begin a second nest may chase the young relentlessly. If there's enough room in the aviary, they will stop chasing after a day or two; by then the young have learned they aren't wanted any longer. Sometimes the parents pluck feathers from the young for a second nest; then they *must* be separated.

Part of the fun of having baby birds is distinguishing them from one another so their personalities show. Small colored plastic bands can be bought from suppliers. Order the correct size for your birds or the bands won't fit correctly. They may be slipped over the bird's leg any time after it has left the nest. They may also be used to mark the parents so you do not confuse pairs of parents and offspring.

The open, slitted side of the plastic band slips over the groove on the banding tool (or on a pair of tweezers if you have no tool). Spread the opening in the band wide enough to fit over the bird's leg. Then the leg is laid into the groove of the tool, the band is held against the leg, and the tool slipped away. Gently press the band closed until it won't slip off yet slides easily up and down on the leg.

A rare triumph for a breeder: baby cockatoos

The closed bands often found on birds bought in stores are used by breeders to tell the age and lineage of a bird. Bird societies issue them to members. Closed bands fit over a bird's foot when it is only a few days old and should be used only by experienced handlers. Another type of band is being placed on birds in quarantine stations. The USDA (United States Department of Agriculture) which regulates the importation of birds is requiring the use of a nylon band that cannot be removed even by psittacines.

If you are successful in raising birds, you can help others learn to do it better if you share your knowledge. Many places will print what you write. Try your school or town newspaper. A local bird club may also want to share in your discoveries. People who are trying to breed better birds read *American Cage Bird Magazine, Bird World, The AFA Watchbird,* and other publications on birds, so you can send your story to one of them, too.

The things you discover about breeding birds could be important. No one knows when all nations will stop the export of native birds or when all species will be banned from importation into the United States. It could happen soon. (See Chapter 14.) Then the only pet birds left in this country will be the ones bred here. Your bit of knowledge about breeding might enable another child to own the same species you have loved enough to breed.

13

HOW TO AVOID PROBLEMS

Birds are really healthy creatures, and if fed the right foods and kept clean, they will live for many years. A bird's worst enemies are dirty water and a dirty cage. You also help protect your bird if you learn as much as possible about its behavior so you notice if something starts to annoy it.

A dim light at night acts as a protector in the dark. Use a shielded light bulb or a seven-watt red bulb sold as a night-light. The diamond doves in my aviary often panic and thud to the floor at night, startling all the other birds into flight. A night-light helps them find their roosting niches again; otherwise they would have to sleep wherever they fell. A sick bird will huddle next to the light bulb for warmth, and you'll find it there in the morning, still alive, but looking for your help.

A bird who seeks a warm place to sleep may simply be molting. Birds use a lot of energy to grow new feathers when they molt. They tend to hop around less than usual to conserve their strength at this time. Usually they stop singing, too. In the wild, birds molt before they migrate and before they raise young, so they are in top condition for these two important events in their lives. Most birds in cages molt twice a year, too, but one molt is partial and hardly noticeable. If fluffy feathers flutter about in the bottom of the cage, your bird is molting.

While it molts, ruffled patches and rakish feathers give a bird an unkempt look. Soon silver streaks appear in its plumage. These are pin feathers not yet unfurled from the sheath. They will burst open into colored feathers before long.

Molting is a gradual process; a few feathers are replaced at a time. Occasionally a bird loses all of its flight feathers at once and cannot fly for a week or two. It will manage quite well hopping and climbing about its cage. The complete process of molting takes about six weeks.

The time of year that birds molt varies with the species. Canaries molt during the summer. Cockatiels, budgerigars, and other parakeets molt during the fall. Australian finches (which include zebra finches) molt late in the summer because the breeding season in their native land coincides with our autumn. Birds who were bred in captivity may molt at a different time of year from what is normal for the species, but they will molt regularly at the same time each year.

A bit of extra care at molting time makes the process easier for a bird. You might want to cover one end of the cage with a towel to be sure the bird has protection from a sudden draft. It is more susceptible to drafts when it is molting. A bird may seem antisocial because it prefers to be left alone at this time. Some birds—budgies, for example—need extra oats. Many breeders add vitamins and minerals to the diet. Actually the best protection for a bird is to feed it the right diet all year long. Then it has built up reserve strength. Most experts don't recommend any change in a canary's diet, for example, though they do suggest feeding canaries cucumbers because they speed the process of molting.

"Color food," sold commercially, contains carotenoids, the red to yellow pigments which give feathers their color. This food enhances colors already within the pigmentation of the feathers, but cannot change nature's true color. Red-factor canaries, for example, need color food to retain their brilliance. A yellow canary's feathers can be made a deep orange by feeding enough of this food, but its offspring will still be yellow because the natural makeup of the feathers has not been altered.

Sometimes problems arise with molting. An especially heavy molt that lasts more than six weeks will weaken a bird. You might want to consult a vet if this happens. An out-of-season molt—which may be an extra molt—can be induced by too much heat or an overlong day caused by artificial lights. A pet store in a mall in Arizona had lights on all night, and the birds in the store molted frequently. Obviously this is hard on the birds. If a cage contains a pair of birds and one is in molt, the other bird may be too active for the comfort of the molting one. Then it would be wise to separate the two birds until the molting is complete.

Feather plucking should not be confused with molting. When you keep moré than one bird in a cage or aviary, they buddy up whether they are mates or not. They sit together and preen and pick at each other. Sometimes one bird starts to look scruffy or may lose feathers on its neck or head—pulled out by its buddy. Diversions—toys, salt spools, treats, millet sprays—may give the birds enough to do to solve the problem, but larger quarters, a chance to build nests (even if the birds are not mates), and some greenery in which to play helps most of all. If nothing works, you will have to separate the birds.

Sometimes feather plucking is temporary. A green singing finch will sit with its chin tucked as it pulls feathers from its chest to line a nest. The expert feather-snatcher in my aviary is a scaly-crowned weaver that will waylay a zebra finch to grab a mouthful of feathers for its nest. A large supply of shredded burlap furnishes a soft nesting material so birds no longer feel the need to pluck feathers. An offending scavenger can also be confined to its own quarters for nesting.

Any birds who feed their mates as part of the courtship ritual—budgies, lovebirds, parrotlets, canaries, are just a few who do—can end up dying for love. It is best to keep cocks and hens in separate cages.

When introducing one bird to another, put both birds into a new cage neither has "owned" before. Even a bird who is anxious for a mate may defend its territory and chase the intruder.

Whenever you want to add a bird to an aviary, buy a bird that will live peaceably with the others you already own. Ask breeders or study the books listed in the appendix to discover the bird's nature. It is sometimes difficult to add a single bird to a colony of birds that has already established a pecking order. The intruder invariably starts at the bottom. If you add two or three birds at a time, the adjustment goes more smoothly. Never add a bird to a colony after nesting has begun; it might upset every bird there and make some desert their eggs.

A multitude of small things, if not avoided, can cause a bird to be sick or to die. Medication should be used with caution and only as a veterinarian directs. Vitamins, for example, if not purified for human use, can cause sickness; so can rancid cod-liver oil. Birds have become ill by chewing on redwood shavings. Kitty litter, sometimes used on the floor of parrots' cages, emits dust that irritates the nasal passages. A tight leg band that won't slip up and down on a bird's leg may cause swelling and pain. When a bird won't *land* on a sore foot, it is a danger signal; something is wrong with its leg or toes. *Standing* on one foot is natural; birds usually sleep that way.

Overcrowding also causes sickness in birds. As a general rule finches and budgies (or any small birds) need about a cubic foot per bird in an aviary. Larger birds need more room.

Pests of various sorts cause troubles, too. Mites suck a bird's blood; you can see the red, swollen creatures on a white cloth thrown over the cage during the night. Lice in the nest may kill babies. Prevention is so much easier than the cure. Just keep the place clean with a weekly washing with chlorine bleach and water. A bird should be transferred to a different cage so you can sterilize its usual one. After cleaning the cage set it outside in the sunshine, which also helps kill pests.

Do not spray every week with a mite and lice spray because the pests build up an immunity to it. If you discover mites have infested the cage, sterilize everything and *then* spray. Change sprays from time to time to prevent pests from building an immunity to the one you use. *Always* read the label on the can.

A bad infestation of mites or lice may require more drastic measures. Remove the bird from the room and hang No Pest Strips in it. After a day or two remove the strips, let the room air for another two or three days, and then the bird can return to its quarters. If you go on vacation and your bird visits a friend at the same time, you can decontaminate its room while you are away. If you keep seed in mouse-proof containers and clean up loose seed in the bird's room, you won't attract bugs and rodents.

In spite of your best care a bird may become sick. Puffy feathers, sluggishness, a collection of excrement under the tail, dull eyes, all point to sickness. The one cure that works with birds is *warmth*. The bird should be moved to a small cage that has a single perch, food and water it can eat without moving off the perch, and a warm place to sleep.

The "special care" cage should be smaller than minimum size for the species. The perch should be across the middle or at one end, close to the floor—so the bird's tail just clears the bottom. Spread seed on the cage floor and fasten a cup of it at one end of the perch. Mount an automatic water feeder so the lip is at floor level, and mount another one at the same end of the perch as the seed cup. A sick bird may sit on the floor, which is why the food should be there, too. Supply grit and a cuttlebone. Add some of the bird's favorite treats to entice it to eat. Mealworms, moistened whole wheat bread, mashed sweet or white potatoes, or squash, are soft foods it may eat if it refuses seed. When the cage is ready, catch the bird and set it gently inside. Catch it swiftly, as a long chase may kill it. A bird should be *alone* in a special care cage. Don't add a mate for company. The cage should be in a room where nothing will disturb the bird.

A heating pad or a light bulb or a very warm room supply the needed warmth. The temperature should be ninety to ninety-five degrees F (thirty-two to thirty-five C) inside the cage. Raise the temperature slowly—about ten degrees an hour. If you use a heating pad, it can be laid across the roof of the cage or under a layer of paper towels on the floor.

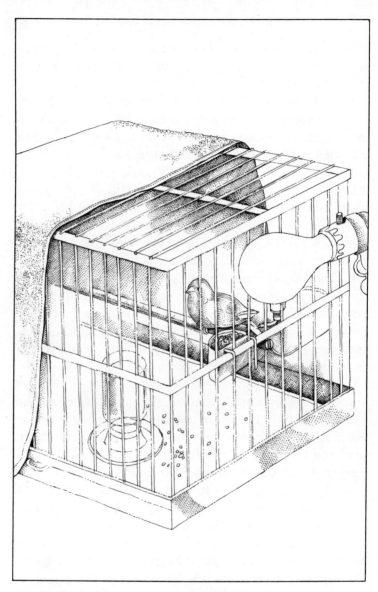

A bulb by the bars for heat and light, food and water close to the perch, and a low bar to sit on make a "special care" cage for a sick bird.

If you use a lamp, rest the bare bulb against the metal bars of the cage at one end of the perch. Start with a twenty-five watt bulb, but if the bird snuggles against it, change to a sixty-watt bulb. Don't go higher than this. A lamp can be placed in a box under the cage instead, which makes the cage warm but also allows the bird to have a normal day and night. Whatever method you use, the warmth must continue twenty-four hours a day every day.

Cover the cage with a bath towel on three sides and the roof but leave the fourth side open so the bird can see the world. The towel must be tucked carefully away from any bulb you use; a fire may start if they touch.

You may buy a commercial hospital cage for a bird, though it will be expensive. For a really valuable bird investigate a used incubator for human babies.

High humidity also helps sick birds. Open water dishes will evaporate in the warmth by the cage and supply the extra humidity. Sick birds should not be given baths, however, because they feel cold with damp feathers.

A bird with excrement under its tail should be cleaned before putting it in the special care cage. Dampen the area with warm water, then gently wipe away the dirt with your finger.

Females sometimes have difficulty laying eggs either because the egg has a thin shell or is stuck (egg-binding). Any hen, whether she is mated or not, may lay eggs and have the same trouble. The warmth relaxes them, so they can lay the egg. The high humidity softens the shell, making it easier for the bird to expel the egg.

If your bird hops around perkily, peeps and eats as soon as you release it in the special care cage, you made a mistake—it wasn't sick. If it snuggles up to the warmth of a light bulb or heating pad, it is sick. A sick bird usually recovers in two or three days, but it could take a week or more. Always leave a bird in the special care cage at least twenty-four hours, even if it becomes perky again. A hen who lays her egg, for example, will act normal and healthy almost immediately, but she should have a period to rest and recover just the same. Lower the temperature in the cage gradually to normal after the bird is well. It should have one full day at a normal temperature before it is returned to its own cage or aviary.

Do not rush a bird off to the vet the instant it looks sick. A car trip may drain the last of its energy and kill it. Consult the vet first, while the bird rests in its special care cage. If the trip is absolutely necessary, confine the bird to a small, dark container and keep it especially warm every minute of the way.

Birds may die suddenly and without reason. A sick bird who is about to die may peck frantically at seeds on the floor, making you think it has begun to recover, only to die a few hours later. A dying bird pants with its bill open and its eyes closed. Its eyes stay open if it pants from fright or the heat.

When a bird dies, you may wonder what to do with it. The body should be burned or buried so it will not contaminate any other living thing. Don't flush it down the toilet or dump it in the rubbish.

Only a vet can tell you if a bird will never recover and should be put to sleep. Vets give birds an injection which kills them painlessly.

Birds always remain fragile, delicate pets. Although your bird may seem to be unlike any other in the world, another bird of the same species will be so similar, it will make a heartwarming substitute. Remember this if your pet dies. It is far easier to find identical birds than identical dogs. Even families with tame birds have found another tame bird takes away the sense of loss. Coco, a zebra finch, flew away into the sunshine one winter day when she accidentally rode outdoors on the collar of someone's coat. Her replacement, a silverbill, brought an entirely new kind of joy with the same endearing tameness, but a whole new character for the family to explore. A more beautiful, more kindly, and tamer bird may be just at hand if you lose your own—so cheer up and go hunting for it.

14

SMUGGLING AFFECTS YOU

Smugglers live to earn a profit on other people's greed. Bird collectors want rare birds, and the more difficult it is to buy one, the more they will pay. The nations of the world have formed a Convention on International Trade in Endangered Species of Wild Fauna and Flora, which publishes the Endangered Species List. When a bird is threatened with extinction in its native land and is added to the list, it cannot be bought or sold legally. New birds are continuously added to the list because people destroy their natural habitat, hunt them, or eat them. Collectors will pay high prices to smugglers to own some of these rare birds. But only a few smugglers could stay in business supplying these rare birds to customers in the United States.

Smugglers also deal in common birds. All birds that enter the United States legally go into quarantine for thirty days. They are tested for Newcastle, a bird disease. A special kind of Newcastle (usually called "exotic" Newcastle) is one hundred percent fatal to poultry, but not to many other species. These other species can be carriers, however, and transmit the disease to other birds. The quarantine services performed by import stations protect the poultry industry in the United States. But it is expensive. Smugglers bypass the import stations and sell their birds for cheaper prices than would be paid for birds that were sold legally.

Smuggled birds may also carry other diseases such as Ornithosis, or Psittacosis (parrot fever), a bacterial disease. People are susceptible to it; fortunately it has a simple cure.

Many South American parrots and budgerigars raised in Mexico cross the Mexican border illegally. It is difficult to patrol the hundreds of miles of border. The many inlets in the Florida coast attract smugglers in boats. An outbreak of Newcastle in Virginia in 1980 suggests that no state is safe from smugglers' activities. Penalties for smuggling are too small to discourage people from trying and trying again.

Smugglers also collect birds in countries that ban the export of their native species. Australia was one of the first nations to pass laws to protect its birds. Many nations are following Australia's example. Only fifteen to twenty percent of the countries that permitted the export of native wildlife three years ago still permit it today.

The biggest demand for smuggled birds comes from people who want a tame, talking bird—especially a parrot. Imported baby parrots that are young enough to tame cannot reach the market (the pet stores and dealers) legally. It takes too long for a parrot to go through the various quarantine procedures; it would be too old to tame by the time it reached the buyer.

It is easy to think you would never buy a smuggled bird yourself. I know someone who visited a place where birds are sold wholesale to stores and dealers around the country. Four young parrots clambered up her coat and sat on her shoulder. She knew they must have been taken from the nest and flown directly to this country to be so young and so tame. She was sure they had been smuggled. If you want a tame parrot more than anything else, it would be difficult to shove one of those babies off your coat and walk away.

But those smuggled birds could carry disease. One bird can start an epidemic of Newcastle disease. If a bird is discovered with the disease, all birds which have come in contact with it are destroyed by the U. S. government. The epidemic in California from 1971 to 1973 resulted in the death of twelve million birds and cost $56 million in payments to owners for compensation. Over a year ago a dealer was found with smuggled, sick birds. Shops in five states had all their birds destroyed because they had come from that one dealer. In San Diego alone 7,500 birds were killed. If you bought a bird that had been contaminated in this way, it, too, would have to be destroyed.

The desire to possess something wild, rare, and beautiful is the source of bird problems. It is estimated that a hundred million wild birds are trapped each year to satisfy the worldwide demand for pet birds. Thousands of birds are imported into the United States each year. Eighty percent of them were captured in the wild in the forests and fields of their native lands. The cruelest part of the bird business lies in this phase of the trade. The wild birds sold legally as well as illegally were captured by trappers.

Some trappers use nets to snare birds on the ground while they eat scattered grain. Others climb trees to find babies in the nest—especially parrots. In some countries trappers cut down the trees in order to raid nests eighty or ninety feet above the ground. When forests are cut this way, a whole cycle of animal and bird life is destroyed for decades to come. Trappers sometimes kill the mothers when capturing the offspring. Birds can also be caught by smearing a sticky substance on tree limbs so birds that lands on the trees cannot fly away. Some birds beat themselves to death trying to escape.

The trappers are paid only a small price for birds, so they do not value them highly. The birds are often kept in crowded cages, fed the wrong kind of food or too little food and no water. They are sometimes injured. A young man who now operates a children's zoo once joined the peace corps in South America. When the natives discovered he knew a lot about birds, they brought birds to him that needed help. Some birds had their wings cut to the bone and didn't have a feather in place. Some had been pinioned and starved. The traumas suffered by wild birds who are caught take the lives of many and blight the future of others.

Since the establishment of import stations in the United States, pressure has been put on trappers to ship healthier birds, which makes the trappers take better care of the ones they catch. The importers want to avoid sick birds that could endanger the entire shipment. In an effort to eliminate these birds, most shipments are held in quarantine in foreign countries for as much as forty-five days.

Legally imported birds spend thirty days in quarantine in the United States. Since import stations were designed for the purpose of preventing the spread of Newcastle to this country, the stations are not equipped to deal with specialized diets or birds that are sick from trauma and travel. Birds that are given the antibiotic to control ornithosis often die from the effects of the antibiotic after leaving the station. Although private import facilities have helped save birds' lives, in any quarantine station where a bird is found to have Newcastle disease, all the birds that were housed with it are humanely destroyed or returned to the country of origin.

No one knows for sure exactly how many birds die after they have been captured and before the time they might have been sold in a pet store. But some die in each stage of their trip: in trappers' cages, in transport, in foreign quarantine stations, in United States import stations, and even, unfortunately, as a result of the changes and fears they have suffered, after arriving safely in peoples' homes. Estimates of the death toll range anywhere from thirty percent to eighty percent of all wild caught birds.

Aviculturalists around the world are working to change this picture. The American Federation of Aviculture is committed to the preservation and captive breeding of endangered species. Experienced breeders in zoos and universities and private breeders across the country are learning to raise many of these birds in captivity. In some cases they are so successful, offspring have been released into the wild to start their own breeding colonies. Your own efforts to breed birds will help to multiply the number in captivity. This helps increase the stock for everyone. The more successful you are, especially with the shier species, the greater your contribution to aviculture will be. This is the challenge!

Another organization, the International Bird Institute, is working to reduce the death toll among imported birds. The members also work with the government in passing regulations to help birds.

The Convention on International Trade in Endangered Species has the objective of "eventually limiting the keeping of pets to those species which can be bred in captivity." This is a promise for the future. An embargo on the import and export of all birds is anticipated soon in the United States. Major importers are already setting up breeding ranches to preserve stock for the pet industry of tomorrow.

It can only be hoped that the U. S. government will be wise enough to permit breeders who have proved their ability to breed hard-to-raise birds to acquire breeding pairs, thereby helping to preserve endangered species. When a total ban on importing birds is established, it should march hand in hand with strict measures to stop smuggling. Otherwise the smugglers will profit the most.

The need for wise buyers will be just as great as it is today. If everyone who wanted a bird for a pet would temper his desire for the rarest species and buy instead a domestically raised bird, smugglers could no longer exist. Wild birds would be safe and free. There would be no need for import stations.

The way to begin is to avoid buying a smuggled bird. Buy directly from a good breeder or reputable pet store. The store or bird farm should be immaculate, the birds sleek and bright-eyed. Beware of cheap prices. Never buy a bird from someone who sells out of a van—this is how smugglers operate. Learn which birds are on the Endangered Species List by reading *American Cage Bird Magazine, Bird World,* and *The AFA Watchbird* so you will recognize if one of these birds is for sale. If you suspect a bird is smuggled, you can call the United States Department of Agriculture at a special number, 301-436-8061.

15

BIRDS OUTSIDE THE WINDOW

The world of wild birds lies at your fingertips. It is as close as the eaves of the house, the park, or the woods and fields beyond the city limits. Cock a watchful eye at the birds while holding a field guide in your hand. The two easiest guides to use come in paperback: Robbins's *Birds of North America* and Peterson's *A Field Guide to the Birds*. Books with maps showing habitats of birds and migration patterns help you to disregard birds who never fly through your state. Know the joy of drawing birds close by hanging a feeder outside the window. Birds become more intimate friends if you lure them to nest in a box you have built.

Getting started as a birder may seem difficult, but others who love birds give a helping hand. A local ornithologist's newspaper column may provide vivid descriptions of the nearby birds. A quick check in your bird guide will lock the picture in your mind, until as the bird flashes past, you know its name. You'll find a welcome at the local Audubon Society, nature museum, or bird preserve. Ask your local librarian how to get in touch with these organizations.

When you are learning to identify birds, try repeating to yourself exactly what the bird looks like while it sits in front of you. Note distinguishing marks that tell birds apart: wing bars, which look as if white splotches had been smeared on the wings; a light-colored ring circling the eye; the color of the legs and bill; the shape of the bill; the shape and length of the tail; flashes of color that only show when the bird flits through the air. The color and size, which *seem* so important, come at the bottom of the list. If you can remember the song and where you saw the bird—in a pine tree, by the shore, in tall grass— your task of finding it in the bird guide will be simplified.

A bird on the feeder often hangs there long enough to give you a good look. A feeder forms a bribe to call birds close enough to watch. If you scatter grain and cracked corn on the ground, you attract the ground-feeders, the birds that eat only off the ground. Since there is no substitute for grains in the wild in snowbound country, if you stop feeding the ground-feeders or miss a day, they may starve. Sunflower seed, one of the most popular seeds with birds, is usually fed in hanging feeders. It is not essential to feed it daily, because the birds that eat it can find other foods in the wild. Of course, if you feed the birds irregularly, they may stop coming to your window. In the South many shy birds may be lured into view by ground feeding. Bobwhites, for example, so often heard but not seen, can become so accustomed to eating grain at a feeder close to high grass, you may see them parade a column of young to the feast.

When a snowstorm howls outside your warm house, think of the birds huddling in a cranny, burning up the last meal for energy to keep warm. Soak some seedless raisins or currants while the storm lasts, drain them as the wind dies down, then pop them outside for the birds. They need this quick energy food as soon as possible. Though you may not feed wild birds as a rule, remember them after a snow or ice storm. If you have no raisins, look in the cupboard for something you can spare: stale bread, nuts cracked open for tiny bills, popcorn, cooked eggs, or even seed from your pet bird.

One of the best ways to save birds' lives in a storm is to leave a box turned on its side on the ground or on top of a woodpile. Place it with the bottom to the wind. Scatter corn on the side that lies flat to the ground. The birds will discover it quickly. If it snows all night, the birds will have feasted at dawn, and when you wake you will see their tracks in the snow and know you saved some lives.

A varied menu will attract a variety of birds. Cracked corn, which is easier to eat than whole kernels, makes one of the finest cold-weather foods. Buy the native, bright yellow variety, not the pale kafir corn so often found in wild bird seed bags. Hunt around for a feed, hardware, garden, or natural food store that sells all sorts of seeds out of sweet-smelling bins. Mix up your own batch of seeds with some oats, wheat, millet, and a smattering of peanut hearts. Add thistle for the birds who come from far to nibble it, and sunflower or safflower seeds.

A mixture of one part honey to four parts water, used to feed pet birds, will also attract hummingbirds. In California and the Rocky Mountains, where so many species abound, as well as in the East which only has the ruby-throated hummingbird, fruit may be offered to attract these flighty, colorful birds.

Suet from the butcher at the supermarket will draw

different types of birds your way. You can make your own with bacon and other drippings, then mix in corn-meal to give substance to the fat. Peanut butter, a most nutritious food, should be mixed with cornmeal or fat so a hungry bird who takes a big bite won't choke on it. Now and then you can supply a bit of bird gravel, because wild birds like grit, too. They will peck happily at egg-shells (but boil them twenty minutes first). Leftovers such as doughnuts and dried bread or cake have less nutritional value than your seed mixture but make easy-to-feed tidbits on the side.

Although there are different species in different sections of the country mingling with birds found almost every-where, the types of food placed in feeders are much the same. Local Audubon Societies usually sell seed mixtures that will help and attract birds in your area.

It may sound odd, but water can be a problem to birds with all that snow around. Until the water freezes, they will drink from a bowl or an automatic feeder like the one for your indoor birds. Fresh water may also attract birds in some coastal areas where salt water abounds.

Wild bird feeders may be shaped in the oddest ways and cost fancy amounts. E-Z-FIL, so good for an aviary indoors, makes an inexpensive feeder outdoors, too. It doesn't clog or spill and keeps the food dry (if you clean the tray from time to time). If a bird could choose its own windowsill feeder, it would ask for glass on the sides so it could watch for approaching enemies in every direction. If you don't want to stand outside shivering while you fill the feeder, buy one that opens easily even when clogged with snow.

You can make your own feeders. A platform feeder can be made with a square piece of wood; the raised edge is formed by strips of wood nailed on the sides. A few

Simple outdoor feeders. Two show ways to discourage squirrels.

holes drilled through the board will drain off melted snow and rain. It can be mounted on a pole or a tree stump.

A narrow log with bark on it turns into a suet or peanut butter feeder if you drill holes a couple of inches deep in the sides. Hang it by one end to an eave or a limb. When you fill it, press the suet in hard so a hungry woodpecker doesn't snap it out in one big bite. The string bags holding lemons, oranges, or onions at the supermarket are transformed into suet packages when hung outdoors. A downy woodpecker may cling there with ease while it bangs away with hammerlike thuds on a frosty day.

A plastic yogurt carton, a wooden salad bowl your mother doesn't want any more, or half a coconut can be suspended as if it were a plant holder—only load it with seed. Two young girls I know cut a large hole in the side of a gallon milk jug, tucked a rusted teaspoon up the spout for hanging it on a wire, and turned it into a feast table when full of seed. It could also become a drinking fountain if filled with water.

Nectar eaters, those birds with long, thin bills who poise in flight above flowers, will drink from a tiny bowl. The bowl becomes an automatic feeder if you invert a bottle over it so the mouth of the bottle just touches the surface of the liquid in the bowl. A hamster water bottle will also serve as a nectar feeder. An orchard owner in California reaped a reward for feeding hummingbirds at feeders on his trees. A plague of insects invaded the area one year, but the birds kept *his* orchard pest-free. For you just the sight of a ruby-throated hummingbird may be reward enough.

Squirrels, those ingenious tightrope walkers, roof climbers, and leapers lunge for feeders wherever they are hung. Wire for hanging pictures—the type with many strands twisted together—will stretch from tree to tree or tree to house without breaking. The feeder should be suspended from the middle of the wire at least three and a half feet above ground (higher than a squirrel can leap). Squirrels trip, slip, and fall if beads are strung on the wire or plastic tubes or hoses surround it. A series of phonograph records—three deep, one above the other —over the feeder cause squirrels to slip climbing down to a feeder. Some Tanglefoot, an evil-smelling repellent, can be smeared on the top record, and the squirrels will only step once in the mess before avoiding it. Do not put Tanglefoot at the edge of a record because birds will cling there.

A metal pole makes climbing difficult. If a metal cone or a metal cover from a garbage pail is suspended near the top of the pole, a squirrel cannot climb over it to reach the feeder on top.

Though bird watchers battle to keep squirrels off their feeders, most of them pity the squirrels, too, and disperse a cheaper seed on the ground. The squirrel population is dropping rapidly in many states due to man, of course, who cuts down nut trees and invents squirrel-proof feeders! Liberal ground offerings solve the feeder problem. Dampened dog food, chicken mash, cracked corn, and wild bird seed scattered widely in the area away from the feeder not only tempts the squirrels away but lures bluejays and starlings to easier pickings. A platform feeder or a table with this type of food will give you hours of watching pleasure.

Think of the window you look out most often—usually where you eat, but sometimes near a chair or desk where you read or study. A feeder hung outside that window will bring a parade of birds before your eyes. Since wet seed turns moldy and other foods spoil, clean the feeder often.

Face the feeder away from the blast of the wind. If you have a choice of sites, pick a southern exposure. More birds will flock to the feeder if shrubs and trees provide places to hide nearby. If you have no trees, try building a brush pile. Birds will feel the area is hospitable and come more frequently if wild berry bushes— blackberry, raspberry, blueberry, currant—give them treats during the growing months. They also like fruit and nut trees, grape vines, and honeysuckle.

If you begin feeding the birds when the fall migrations reach your area, you will have a wide variety of birds at your feeder all fall and winter. During spring and fall migrations, Southerners can help preserve rare song birds by offering a variety of seeds in their feeders.

Your indoor bird may help woo the outdoor birds to your window. My husband's and my aviary full of foreign finches in a house in Maine attracts the fall warblers— northern yellowthroats, ovenbirds, Nashville warblers— who hang outside the windows as if asking the indoor finches to come out and play.

If the nesting cycle of birds holds a fascination for you, the wild birds might be persuaded to nest in your backyard. The nesting box needs to be the right size and in the right location to attract birds to it. Two birds— the house wren and the chickadee—adapt willingly to houses built by people. A nesting box four by four inches on the bottom and eight inches high, with a second choice nearby a bit larger (four by six inches on the bottom) might bring an eager house wren to its door. The entrance hole should be six inches high on one side and a bit of a squeeze sizewise for the tiny wren: one and an eighth inch diameter—the size of a quarter. A box mounted on a post or pole pleases the choosy parent most, but some will accept one hanging in a tree if it doesn't swing around too much. Earth color—drab—for the paint lets the box blend into its surroundings. The spot you place it should bask in the sun sixty percent of the day.

Chickadees have similar tastes. They'll pick a box in an earth-tone that is four by four by eight inches, or perhaps five by five by eight inches, with the same size hole wrens like. Their box should be mounted only on a pole or post—they do not want to rock their young to sleep in a tree. The box may be in a shadier yard with only forty percent to sixty percent sunshine. Both birds like cover nearby: a handsome pile of brush for wrens will do if there are some shrubs around, too, but chickadees like to have trees as well.

In both the North and the South woodpeckers can often be encouraged to nest in dead trees nearby. It is even possible to erect a dead trunk upright on your property to create a nesting site.

The habitat must be right for other birds. Swallows swoop over the water, nest near it, but want open fields nearby also. Bluebirds have special tastes; they ask for a place with open fields and pasture, woods, hedgerows, an orchard if possible, and tall grass. The Audubon Workshop Catalogue offers bluebird nest boxes for sale. Flickers only nest in large trees. One of the birds who looks desperately for nests and has trouble finding them is the wood duck. It insists on a house the right size close to a pond or slow-moving water.

All small birds except the house wren and chickadee need protection from house sparrows or starlings. House sparrows enjoy the same type of houses as tree swallows, for example, but if the doors to the houses are covered until the swallows arrive, the sparrows will have begun

Help wild birds breed and survive with nesting boxes. *Left:* chickadee; *top right:* wren; *bottom right:* bluebird.

nesting already in other houses. Sometimes sparrows must be ousted from a box and their eggs removed to keep the house vacant for a preferred bird resident.

A student once proved how important habitat can be by choosing bluebirds and house sparrows for his examples. He set up a long row of birdhouses all alike, since they nest in the same kind of house, with one end of the line in open fields and orchards which bluebirds like and the other end in more wooded areas for house sparrows. Sure enough the bluebirds chose houses in their preferred habitat and the' house sparrows chose in theirs. But the house in the middle became a battleground and was fought over so furiously that no young were ever reared in it.

Starlings can be shooed from houses you want other birds to use by nailing a shiny piece of aluminum inside opposite the door. Squirrels can be kept from littering the house with junk if aluminum flashing is mounted on the underside of the house or on the post beneath it.

Once you have become a birdwatcher, you notice birds in trouble. It is tempting to go to their aid and bring them into the house. This is not only dangerous for your pet bird, who will be exposed to the sick bird, but it is illegal. No one is allowed to keep a native bird in captivity in the United States. Specialists who understand birds may obtain a license to keep birds for study and other reasons. Children under eighteen cannot obtain a license to keep wild birds. If a bird has been injured, you should contact a vet or the Audubon Society. Someone who is licensed will give it proper care.

Starlings are one of the few birds anyone may keep in captivity without a license. This species was introduced into the United States from Europe in the nineteenth century. Its numbers have exploded to such proportions, colonies of millions of starlings have been counted roosting together. Starlings are now the most numerous—and unpopular—bird in the country. They crowd out of breeding and feeding grounds many of our native songbirds, so that some are threatened with extinction. Bluebirds are just one of the species starlings have forced away from their habitats.

Government agencies work to protect our native birds. They pass regulations to prevent the importing of birds that might endanger other native species. Our country learned this lesson the hard way with starlings. It is, therefore, against the law to release to the wild any species that is not native to this country.

The government needs the cooperation of pet owners. One of the worst things you can do is to release a pet bird to the wild, either by mistake or because you think it is kind to the bird. The delicate species, finches and canaries, seldom survive in the wild, but the larger birds pose a threat. Thirty-six species of foreign birds have already become established in various states. They have invaded the nesting areas of shier birds, devoured their food supplies, and put some on the endangered species list.

Though you may help wild birds by feeding them or building houses where they may nest, though you have learned to leave nests in the wild alone, you can help even more by gaining knowledge and working through your local Audubon Society (see p. 166). You may help preserve the unique place birds fill in man's world.

Birds are threatened today when people clear meadowland for houses, fill in marshes, cut down forests, make beaches where tidewater once washed, and abandon farmlands. If you read the local newspaper so you know when such projects are planned in your community, you can go to meetings where they are discussed. The voice of the youngest person carries great weight at such meetings because the fate of birds and land is part of your future.

Your knowledge of smuggling, of endangered species lists, and the import stations can be an influence on congressmen and senators who make the laws about importing and exporting.

Misinformation often injures families of birds in the wild. So many people, for example, are ignorant of the place hawks fill in the ecology picture. Hawks cull the flocks of smaller birds by catching the weak and sick ones. If they did not, the smaller birds would deplete their feeding grounds because they multiply so rapidly. There are hawks who live mainly on insects, and ones who eat only small birds. Even the large hawks who can kill chickens live mainly on grouse and other wild game. Yet farmers and hunters and even the average person often have the idea that hawks are evil birds who should be shot on sight. Now many hawks are on the endangered species lists in states where they once swooped in numbers through the sky. Whenever you know the facts that will correct the wrong concept, you may help save the lives of many birds.

When national issues affect wildlife, you can play a part, too. Many pieces of legislation in Congress affect birds in seacoast areas, in national parks, in forest preserves. Letters from young people who are most affected by such legislation can influence congressmen. You will understand these issues better and write with authority if you join the National Audubon Society, a conservation organization. Your ability to help birds will expand with knowledge as a bird's view expands with upward, soaring flight.

APPENDIX I

TABLE I

Finches

Life span: About 8 years with the correct diet, care, and exercise.

Time to buy: Whenever birds are not molting. Australian finches tend to molt in summer, but a hot store may cause out-of-season molting.

Diet: Basic—water, finch seed, finch mineral grit, cuttlebone. Supplements—greens, vegetables, fruit, Petamine, seeding grasses, eggshell, whole wheat bread. High protein foods (ration to birds in cages)—eggs, mealworms.

Cage size: ⅜ inch spacing between bars. Approximate size—8 x 10 x 12 inches. Anything smaller cramps their flying.

Nesting box: 5 inches square. Wicker baskets. Open canary nests.

Nesting material: Shredded burlap from 1-2 inch squares; salt marsh hay; nesting hair; grass.

Easiest species to breed: zebra, society, silverbill.

Finches That Are Easy to Breed

ZEBRA FINCH (*Poephila guttata*)

Origin: Australia.

Availability: Raised in every state; the most common finch.

Nature: A personality bird; peaceable.

Size: 4½ inches.

Song: Similar to the honking of a toy horn.

Color: Normal—gray. Other colors—white, fawn, pied, silver, and many other mutations.

Cost: The cheapest domestically raised bird.

Ease of taming: Will tame within one to three days if it is isolated from other birds and trained before it is four weeks old. Both sexes tame easily.

Sociability: Peaceable in aviaries. They may interfere with the nests of more timid species. Two or more zebras of the same sex may be housed together.

Diet: Finch diet listed above. Niger (thistle) may be fed sparingly, but should be offered freely during the molt. Millet sprays a favorite.

Breeding diet: Eggs, mealworms, greens, nestling food (it may be dry) are fed to young, although zebras will raise young on seed alone. They seldom eat eggs unless they are feeding young.

Breeding: Begin with colony breeding; start with two pairs. Hens should be eight months old (there is less chance of egg-binding if they are allowed to mature). Use finch nesting boxes (5 inches square) with only enough nesting material for one nest. Zebras sandwich nests complete with unhatched eggs. They will incubate and raise the young of other species. It is difficult for them to foster Gouldian finches because these birds take an extra week in the nest. Sometimes if a zebra cock is left alone with the young, he may feed them long enough. Two pairs of zebras may nest together in a flight cage.

Incubation: 12 days (usual). Eggs do not all hatch on the same day.

Fledging: 12 to 14 days after hatching. Parents will continue to feed the young for about two weeks after fledging.

Sexing the young: Gray cocks have flecks of black at the tips of one or two feathers within the first week of fledging. Hens retain a black line below the eye that looks like running mascara. (This line fades on cocks.) By three weeks of age most cocks show enough color on the chest, flanks, and cheeks to be sexed. Cocks begin a raspy song before three weeks old. White zebras can only be sexed by the song or by the line on the hen's face if she has one. When the bills have adult color: cock's is bright red; hen's retains pinkish tinge. The bills change to adult color more rapidly in warm weather and are redder in color in mating season. Even bill color may be deceiving in some cases, because it may be pale in some males, or brighter in some females.

Sexing adults: Cocks in most colors have orange cheek patches. Cocks usually have brighter red bills than adult hens. Most hens, but not all of them, have a black line by the eye. Most cocks (except whites and pies) have more color—chestnut sides and dark markings on the chest—than hens.

SOCIETY FINCH (Bengalese) (*Lonchura domestica*)

Origin: Unknown. Societies were bred—probably from various mannikins, which are a family of birds—in China or Japan so long ago their ancestors are lost in time. None exist in the wild today.

Availability: In some parts of the country as easy to find as zebra finches.

Nature: Peaceful, bouncy. Devoted parents.

Size: 4¼ inches.

Song: Squeaky up and down tune accompanied by puffing of their feathers.

Color: No two are exactly alike. They are a mixture of white with brown (which may appear almost black, light brown, or tan). Many cinnamon and dark brown societies have no white. Pure white is a recessive trait and birds of this color tend toward weakness and possible blindness if overbred. Some have canary-type crests.

Cost: When easily available, same as zebras; otherwise more expensive than zebras.

Ease of taming: They will tame in a few days if trained before four weeks old.

Sociability: Compatible with all finches and with other birds of their own species. They are nonaggressive.

Diet: Zebra diet. They need white millet and canary seed also.

Breeding: Breed almost as easily as zebra finches. They do not need two pairs together to breed. They prefer to breed in an individual cage. They will breed in a mixed aviary if given secluded nesting sites, but they tend to invade other nests to help build or sit on the eggs. Discourage several birds brooding in the same nest because it is bad for the young.

Foster parents: Society finches will incubate and raise the young of other birds, even along with their own.

Young societies who have not yet raised a clutch of their own make the best foster parents. A pair of bachelors have been known to raise young from other birds. Note—when used consistently for raising Gouldians, societies may not be able to raise their own young afterward.

Incubation: 13 days.

Sexing: By behavior. The cock sings a raucous song and performs a courting dance. If each bird is placed in a separate cage in an isolated room for half an hour, when placed side by side again, the cock will sing. If neither bird sings, both are probably, but not positively, hens. More hens than cocks result from breeding.

AFRICAN SILVERBILL (*Euodice cantans*); INDIAN SILVERBILL (*E. malabarica*)

Origin: One species comes from Africa, the other from India.

Availability: Fairly common.

Nature: Nonaggressive, active, entertaining. Wag their tails. Shy.

Size: 4 inches.

Song: Melodious as a waterfall.

Color: Silvery gray birds with silver bills; underparts buffy.

Cost: The same or slightly more than society finches.

Ease of taming: As easy as zebra finches if trained before four weeks old.

Sociability: Compatible with all finches.

Diet: Finch mixture, seeding grasses, millet sprays, eggshells. They are seedeaters, but greens and vegetables may be offered. (Feed all the basic foods.)

Breeding diet: Some insectivorous soft food may be offered.

Breeding: More than one pair will breed in the same aviary. They usually prefer wicker baskets to nesting boxes. Other species may discourage them from nesting.

Incubation: 12-14 days.

Sexing: By behavior. The cock sings tiny tunes—the throat vibrates even if the song is barely audible—before the bird is four weeks old. A silent bird may be a cock, but a singer surely is. Hens have flatter heads than cocks; if the two are side by side, you can sometimes see the more rounded dome on the cock's head. Hens are more flighty than cocks.

Common Finches and Finch-like Birds Bred by Experienced Breeders

The following finches are bred in almost every state, but unless you live in an area where a particular species is bred, it may be rare.

Cost: At least double that of zebra finches, but even within a city it can vary widely for all species.

Diet: Finch diet unless special food is mentioned.

Breeding: Not recommended for amateurs until they prove success with the species mentioned above.

CORDON-BLEU (*Uraeginthus bengalus*)

Origin: Africa.

Nature: Peaceful. A swift-flying, perky waxbill (a finch-like bird).

Size: 4½ inches.

Song: A pretty, short tune. Even hens sing a small song sometimes.

Color: Turquoise. Males have splashes of red on their

cheeks. The buff on the females spreads deeper on the chest than on the males.

Breeding diet: Live food necessary.

CUT-THROAT or RIBBON FINCH (*Amadina fasciata*)
Origin: Africa.
Nature: Hearty birds, but somewhat aggressive. They may pluck the feathers from smaller birds if housed in the same cage or aviary.
Size: 5 inches.
Song: Unusual song accompanied by courtship dance.
Color: A scaly pattern of browns and grays. The male has a splash of red across the throat.
Breeding: They prefer a nesting box a bit larger than zebras use, which is 5 inches cubed.

GOULDIAN FINCH or LADY GOULD (*Poephila gouldiae*)
Origin: Australia.
Nature: Peaceful, quiet, with a highly developed sense of curiosity; delicate.
Size: 5 inches.
Song: So soft it is difficult to hear; a whispering tune.
Color: Often considered the most beautiful of all finches. Seven colors from the purple abdomen to the turquoise neck and red or black or yellow head. Female has paler colors, a softened reflection of the male.
Cost: Expensive. A single Gouldian finch will cost more than a cockatiel.
Diet: Finch mix, growing grasses, fruit and vegetables, scrambled eggs, spray millet, grit, water, cuttlebone (both a whole one and a cupful of scrapings), rock salt. The last two items are considered essential.
Breeding: Best method is colony breeding in a large

flight aviary; but they also nest in single cages. Do not disturb them at all while breeding.

Diet for young: Live food if possible, eggs if the parents refuse to eat live food; oily seeds such as thistle, green pepper seeds, or oil on the finch seed; millet sprays and seeding grasses. This diet helps bring the young through the critical first molt.

GREEN SINGING FINCH (*Serinus mozambicus*)

Origin: Africa.

Nature: One of the heartiest, long-lived, and peaceable finches.

Size: 5 inches.

Song: A bubbling, ear-tingling song; canary-like but shorter than a canary's.

Color: A sparkling yellow bird with olive on its back. The older the bird, the brighter its yellow. Females wear a necklace of gray feathers faintly outlined on the throat.

Breeding: They breed more successfully if an extra male is at hand to spark the nesting of the pair. Cocks sometimes destroy eggs or young in the nest. In this case they should be removed when the hen lays her eggs.

Breeding diet: Live food for young.

Note: Green singing finches often avoid eating off the floor. Live food should be offered above floor level.

LAVENDER FINCH (*Estrilda caerulescens*)

Origin: Africa.

Nature: Friendly (to humans), lots of curiosity, quick-flying, gentle.

Size: 4 inches.

Song: Soft, but pretty.

Color: Soft gray with deep red on the lower back, rump,

and central tail feathers. Both sexes identical color. (Some experts detect more black on the ventral area of males than on females.)

Diet: Especially like mealworms and spray millet.

MANNIKINS; BLACK-HEADED NUN (*Lonchura ferruginosa*), TRI-COLORED NUN (*Lonchura malacca*), WHITE-HEADED NUN (*Lonchura maja*)

Origin: Southeastern Asia.

Nature: Peaceable. Sedentary. Among the less intelligent birds.

Size: 4½ inches.

Song: Some males sing a faint, squeaky song enthusiastically.

Color: A striking appearance due to the sharp division of colors.

Breeding: Nuns, as part of the mannikin family, can crossbreed with other mannikins, but the young are infertile.

note: Their toenails grow long and should be trimmed *at least* four times a year.

ORANGE-CHEEKED WAXBILL (*Estrilda melpoda*)

Origin: Africa.

Nature: A bouncy, active little waxbill that constantly flicks its tail. It has a bright-eyed look as if the world were always a wonder.

Size: 3½ inches.

Song: Small.

Color: Fawn color with bright orange cheeks. Both sexes similar, but female has slightly paler cheeks.

Note: The small waxbills—the orange-cheeked, red-eared, and strawberry finch—take more tender loving care than the larger finches. They should not be bought until the owner successfully keeps larger finches alive. The wax-bills survive better in quarters larger than the usual finch cage.

ORANGE WEAVER, sometimes called BISHOPS (*Euplectes orix franciscana*)
Origin: Africa.
Nature: Hearty, active, but do not mix in aviaries with smaller finches. They chase!
Size: 4 inches.
Song: High-pitched, squeaky.
Color: A Halloween bird with black and orange colors. In the off-season it molts to a drab, sparrow-like brown. Female is always drab brown. Newly imported birds may be red instead of orange. The orange is due to a deficiency in the diet in captivity.

RED-EARED WAXBILL (*Estrilda troglodytes*)
Origin: Africa.
Nature: Inquisitive, quick, similar to orange-cheeked waxbill.
Size: 3½ inches.
Song: Soft.
Color: Soft tan-gray with a rosy red vent and red mark through the eye.

SPICE BIRD or SPICE MANNIKIN (*Lonchura punctulata*)
Origin: Asia.
Nature: Peaceable, quiet.
Size: 4½ inches.
Song: Not often heard singing.
Color: Nutmeg brown, but the chest markings make it striking. Here the feathers are edged with contrasting colors to create a scalloped appearance.

STAR FINCH (*Bathilda ruficauda*)

Origin: Australia.

Nature: Gentle, but determined; active; one of the author's favorite finches.

Size: 4½ inches.

Song: A bit like the zebra finch's, but more melodious.

Color: They have a partyish look with their red masks. Body is chartreuse; the throat yellowish with tiny white dots. Females paler than males.

Diet: Niger (thistle) needed in the diet along with the finch mixture.

Breeding: Although seldom mentioned as easy-to-breed, a little care produces results. Many breeders give the eggs to societies to incubate, but the stars make good parents, too. One pair will keep several pairs of society finches busy raising their young. They cannot be housed with more aggressive birds if you want them to breed. Their nest must not be touched or examined. Incubation and fledging period is similar to zebras.

Breeding diet: They need live food to raise their young.

STRAWBERRY FINCH (*Amandava amandava*)

Origin: There are two races, one in South Central Asia and one in East Asia.

Nature: A bundle of energy; hearty once they are acclimated. Females are difficult to acclimate.

Size: 3½ inches.

Song: A soaring song that glides at the end into a minor key.

Color: Red coloring speckled with white on the cocks. Hens have pale yellow on the underparts and lack the bright red of the cock.

Note: Hens are often subject to egg-binding until well acclimated.

Many other finches may be available locally depending on the breeders in the area. The choice is wider in warmer climates where it is easier to breed in outdoor aviaries.

TABLE II

Popular Psittacines

Psittacines are parrots or parrot-like birds with plump bodies and bills with hooks that are used for climbing and for cracking nuts. Their feet have two toes facing forward and two backward so they can cling to the sides of trees the way woodpeckers do. (Most birds have only one toe facing backward.) The budgerigar and cockatiel are the most common and popular of the hook-bills.

BUDGERIGARS (*Melopsittacus undulatus*)

"Parakeet": A budgerigar is commonly called a "parakeet" in the United States. Actually it is *one* species of Parakeet, which is a whole family of birds with many species on several continents.

Nature: Budgies have a spunky, sassy, determined personality. They enjoy being talked to and thrive on attention.

Life span: About 10 years.

Size: 7½ inches.

Cost: Least expensive psittacine; breeders can be found in every state.

When to buy: Any time except September to November when they molt.

Ease of taming: If bought young, budgies tame easily. It is best to pick one who has just become self-feeding at about six weeks old. It should be less than four months old. One color is not more easy to tame or teach to talk than any other. Females may tame more easily; males are more likely to develop a large vocabulary.

How to pick a young bird: The black lines on the forehead (in most colors) disappear at the first molt, and by then the bird is too old to tame easily. Note the color of the cere. This waxy piece of flesh appears shiny and fleshy; it is above the beak and has two holes (the nostrils) in it. Immature budgies have a light blue or light violet cere.

Sexing: Breeders usually know, though even they can make a mistake. If the cere has a pinkish look that appears a solid shade, it is probably a cock. A pale blue cere with specks of white in it around the nostrils usually means a hen. When startled, the hen's cere will get a paler rim circling the nostrils. A hen's cere is rounder and larger than a cock's, but it takes contrast of seeing both sexes together in order to tell them apart.

In adults—cocks have a blue cere (except lutinos and albinos who have pinkish ones); hens have a brown cere. It may be difficult to tell a young female from a slightly older cock when both have bluish ceres.

Colors: Through cage-breeding budgies have mutated from the wild ones with yellow faces and green bodies. Now they come in a profusion of colors from the rare violet to white, yellow, mauve, sky blue, green, gray.

Minimum size cage: 7 x 10 x 10 inches is standard size. Openings in hardware cloth—½ x 1 inch. Horizontal bars on one to three sides aid climbing.

Perches: ⅝ inch diameter if dowel. Hardwood. Limbs from fruit or hardwood trees are better.

Diet: Basic foods include budgerigar mix (millets, especially white proso millet; canary seed; 5-10% oats), grit (without charcoal), mineral block, water. Supplements include greens (the best are coarse grass, goose grass, stems of heavy lawn grass), millet sprays, fresh bark (limbs from fruit, willow, honeysuckle, hardwoods), and a piece of fruit or vegetable daily. Other possible foods include soybean meal (often 10% of the seed mixture), eggshell, cottage cheese, whole wheat bread.

When molting feed 5% extra oats. Immature budgies should have extra canary seed because they can crack it better than millet, so eat more and grow more quickly.

When a budgie eats its normal droppings (black and white and dry), it wants vitamin B-12, which is manufactured in its body and expelled in the droppings. A food that supplies the vitamin curbs the bird's urge to eat it.

A budgie that is healthy and bouncy but stops singing has come into breeding condition—if you have a tame budgie or one you don't want to breed, cut back on the oats.

Two Budgies: If you buy a second budgie to keep a pet bird company, they will probably fight.

Creepers: When a budgie's wings are clipped to prevent it from flying while you tame it, six to eight of the wing feathers are cut short in an even line, but the two longest outside feathers will be unclipped because it looks prettier. A budgie afflicted with French molt will have rough edges to the wing. Its feathers break off as they form and never grow to full length. The tail will be affected, too. There is no cure. Such birds are often called "creepers" or "runners" because they cannot fly.

Breeding: It is easiest for a beginner to breed in colonies
(start with two pairs) in an aviary. Buy the breeding
pairs young, then wait until they are at least eight
months old to mate them. Four to six weeks before
breeding, condition budgies with extra oats and some
whole wheat bread with a few drops of wheat germ
oil on it. Hens are ready to mate when they bite at bits
of wood and call; their ceres become a deep, rich
brown. Cocks strut, rattle their beaks on the cage bars,
or jiggle the feed cups; cere turns deep, bright blue;
they call loudly. Only then should the cocks and hens
be put together. After they mate, add the nesting boxes.
Nesting box: 7 x 7 x 8 (to 10) inches. Entrance hole 1½
inches. No post under hole. Nesting block 1 inch thick
in bottom hollowed into a cavity to hold the eggs.

Budgies seldom use nesting material, but you can
add a bit of peat moss, sawdust, or seed husks. High
humidity is necessary if the eggs are to hatch. In dry
climates try some blotting paper you keep damp. A
couple of pails of water in the room help (but cover
the tops with screening so birds don't fall in). The
temperature in the room should not go under 50 or over
70 degrees F (10°-21°C).

A clutch runs 4 to 6 eggs (but limit it to 6). Incubation (count from the day the hen goes into the nest to
stay) takes 17 to 20 days. Longer if it is cold. 18 days
is normal.

Do not peek. Stay away and keep feeding time to a
minimum. The parents feed soaked seed to the young.
You can buy a commercial mix at the suppliers. Some
breeders add wheat germ or cod liver oil. The parents
form a milk crop, a thick, soft, cheesy food. They bring
up this curd and stuff it into the babies' mouths. After
the first few days you can risk a cautious peek when

the parents are out eating. Be sure no dead babies lie in the nest. Remove them if there are; the rest will be all right.

Fledging: About 4 weeks.

Weaning: About 6 weeks. Be positive the young eat frequently and a lot at one time before taking them from their parents. Scatter seed on the floor of the weaning cage.

COCKATIELS (*Nymphicus hollandicus*)

Origin: Australia, where flocks of cockatiels are as common as sparrows in the United States.

Nature: Peaceable, gentle, devoted to their owners. Are good mimics. Can entertain themselves when alone, so seldom get moody as parrots can.

Talking ability: A cockatiel should be hand-reared if possible in order to tame easily and talk well. It should be purchased when under four months of age or it is difficult to tame. Both sexes tame and will talk. All learn to whistle. They should learn to talk first, however, or they will not pick up words easily—they enjoy whistling too much.

Compatibility: Peaceable with other cockatiels and even with finches and smaller parrot-like birds.

Life-span: 10 to 14 years. One trouper is 27 and still performing.

Availability: Found in every state. There are many domestic breeders, but cockatiels are still imported in numbers (from foreign breeders, not caught in the wild). A hand-reared cockatiel, however, is more difficult to find. Check *American Cage Bird Magazine, Bird World*, and *The AFA Watchbird* ads.

Cost: Gray cockatiels—four to six times the price of a budgie.

Size: 13 inches.

Colors: Gray is normal; it has a white splash of color on the wings, a long, pointed crest, and yellow with an orange spot in doll-like fashion on the cheeks. Albinos are expensive and may be weak from overbreeding. Pearled (hen brighter colors than cock), pied, cinnamon (Isabell), silver.

Sexing: Adult hens—crest with brownish tinge, less yellow, and the orange paler than on cocks; tail speckled with white. Immatures look alike. It is difficult to sex normal grays when young. A skilled fancier may be able to guess the sex of the male at about five months by noting a few bright yellow feathers on the face.

Baths: Cockatiels like baths at least once a day. Do not spray them with anything except water. Do not use a mite spray on cockatiels. They have a powdery slough, which is a dusty film, on their feathers. It makes the feathers look soft, rather than glossy. A mite spray has an oil base which would mix with the powdery slough and make it gummy.

Minimum cage size: 15 x 24 x 20 inches. A parrot cage acceptable. Cockatiels make strong flyers so need maximum room for exercise daily. Cages should be metal, not wood. Openings between bars an inch square maximum. Cover at night; it gives them a feeling of security.

Toys: Musical perches, ladders, bells, plastic babies, mirrors.

Diet: Begin with a commercial cockatiel mix. Basic seed mix includes canary seed, white proso millet, oat groats, sunflower. Safflower seeds are better for the bird's health if it can be taught to eat them when young. Also feed—water, cuttlebone, mineral block, salt spool, budgie grit (mixed with oyster shell and charcoal).

Supplement diet with tree limbs, bark, greens, fruits and vegetables (they usually like carrots especially), millet sprays, native grasses, raw (shelled) peanuts once a week, whole wheat bread, eggs, crackers, biscuits. For immature birds—if under four months, crack sunflower seeds in the blender or feed kernels. Young birds will eat raw peanut hearts when sunflower seeds are still too hard to crack.

Foster parents: Will raise young of rarer parakeet species.

Breeding: An amateur should begin by colony breeding with two pairs in an aviary. They must be two years old to breed. They are secretive birds, so keep them in a quiet, secluded place. It should be warm (65-70 degrees F, 18-21° C) with a high humidity. Nesting box: 12 inches square by 24 inches high; 3-inch entrance hole. Some like an even larger box. Nesting material: sawdust, cedar shavings, rotted wood, peat moss. Conditioning food may include: whole wheat bread with a few drops of wheat germ oil, commercial condition food, eggs, eggshells, extra minerals and vitamins. Clutch: 4 to 6 (usual) eggs. Incubation: 18 (usual) to 21 days. The parents produce a milk crop to feed the young, so give them plenty of fruits, vegetables (especially carrots and corn). Also: whole wheat bread, oat groats, nestling food. No peanuts while young are being fed, as they may cause a "hard crop," which is usually fatal.

Fledging: They fledge in four to five weeks.

Note: The entire issue of *The AFA Watchbird* of October–November 1978 was devoted to cockatiels, including breeding, taming, and care.

Do not handle young birds for the first couple of weeks. You may be able to hold them occasionally after that if the parents are away from the nest and do not catch you doing it. A startled father could hurt the babies, so be careful. Professionals can handle the babies even sooner, but learn how to breed the birds first before you experiment with taming them in the nest.

TABLE III

Canaries

Domestic canaries originated with the wild canary (*Serinus canaria*). This small greenish bird gave little hint of the song potential that would be developed through careful breeding in captivity.

Origin: Canary islands, Madeira, and the Azores.

Availability: Bred in every state.

Nature: Canaries are enjoyed for their color, song, and personality. Rollers come in many shades of color. The American singer, whose song has developed into vibrant variations, sings more frequently than any other variety, including rollers, and is especially adaptable to family living in a city apartment. More choppers, a loud-singing bird that is bred abroad, are sold in pet shops.

Colors: White (a true white, not albino, which has red eyes), red factor (in colors from pale pink to deep red-orange), with many shades in between.

Types: A great number of variations exist. Among them —crested canary (with a mop-top), Yorkshire (stylish, slim), roller canary (song canary).

Size: Varies with the type. May be no more than 4½ inches or as long as 7¾ inches.

Cost: Varies greatly depending on how many breeders are in the area.

Cage size: Standard canary cage. No smaller than 7 x 7 x 10 inches.

When to buy: Canaries molt during July, August, and September, so do not buy one at this time. The baby molt finishes at six months of age, so do not buy one younger than this. It is better to wait until it is eight months old.

Sexing: Males sing with a *swollen* throat, a consistent, full song. Females may sing a little tune, but it is short and ends with a jerk of the head. Experts tell by blowing feathers off the vent—if the vent follows the breast-line, i.e.: the vent does not protrude—it is a hen; if it is extended slightly and follows the tail, it is a cock. When out of breeding condition, cocks are indistinguishable from hens.

Compatibility: Mated pairs of canaries mix in a colony. Female canaries tend to bully smaller finches.

Diet: Canary seed (canary seed and rape), water, cuttlebone, canary grit, Petamine, greens (may include dandelions, chickweed). Supplements may include millet (in the milky stage only), small amounts of fruits and vegetables (too much thins the song), nasturtiums for color, cucumbers for molting. Oats only if bird is in a cold room (under 50 degrees F, 10° C) or has lots of exercise flying. Some breeders feed flax to molting birds. Egg—for show cocks; for parents feeding young; most breeders do not feed eggs regularly. Thistle—part of basic diet for red-factor canaries. If a canary stops singing, it may be coming into breeding condition. It will sing again if you stop feeding all rich foods, shorten the day and lower the temperature.

Breeding: Canaries should be bred in the spring. To condition them feed wheat germ oil, crushed eggshells, and oats to hens; oats to cocks. Wheat germ oil may be fed on whole wheat bread or mixed with egg and condition food. This conditioning is usually begun in mid-January. Add extra light to the day gradually by artificial lights before sunrise. Maintain 70-degree F, 21 degree C, temperature. (It may drop a bit at night.) Colony breeding in an aviary is easier for the amateur.

Canaries are delicate, temperamental birds who demand a regular schedule for meals and protection from noises, strangers, disturbances at night, and peeking. When the cock is ready to mate, he sings loudly, is restless, and feeds the hen through the bars that separate them. The hen carries feathers around in her bill and calls back to the cock. When they are both ready to mate, they may be released together into the aviary. Supply the birds with canary (open) nests and gradually add nesting hair. The hen builds the nest. A clutch of 4 to 5 eggs is normal. Stop feeding wheat germ oil when first egg is laid. Remove each egg (let it roll onto a spoon) and replace it with a dummy egg. Wait until hen is out of the nest to switch the eggs. Carefully lay the eggs in a small box full of seed or seed husks, which act as a cushion so they won't break. The eggs are removed so the young will hatch at the same time. If they hatched on successive days the last chick to hatch would be too small to compete for food. The eggs keep safely without extra warmth. Replace the eggs on the morning of the fourth day (or evening of the third). When eggs are returned to the nest, breeders say they have "set" the hen. Incubation takes 13 to 14 days. On twelfth day add a small amount of nestling food in case one egg hatches early. Give no baths until the twelfth day, but then lure the hen into the water with a bit of lettuce in the bath. Her damp feathers soften the eggshells, making it easier for young to peck free. Eggs may be dampened with ¼ teaspoon of warm water.

When the young hatch, the hen must be lured away from the nestlings to get food to feed them. Use her favorite treat. If she won't leave the nest because the male has been feeding her and she's waiting for him, take him away until she goes for food. Spend as little time as possible feeding and cleaning up the first few critical days.

Breeding Diet: Fresh nestling food mixed with egg, changed four times a day to prevent spoiling. Never leave any in the cage overnight. First feeding in the morning must be at dawn—set your alarm. A nestling food may be bought from suppliers. Breeders sometimes add grated carrots, soybean milk powder, gelatin or powdered milk to nestling food. Once you start a formula, do not change it. The cock feeds a milky substance the first few days and needs extra water to manufacture it. Feed plenty of food as young grow.

Canaries fledge in 16 to 20 days. Put a cap of seed and one of nestling food on the floor for them. Crack seed for them in the blender until they are six weeks old. Weaning is at 28 to 30 days. Be sure young are self-feeding before removing them from the parents. If the hen starts a second nest before young are weaned, put young on the other side of a partition where hen can still feed them through the bars but cannot pluck their feathers for her nest. At six weeks of age chicks should be on seed only (no more nestling food) and eating an adult diet including greens.

Crosses: Canaries have been mated to green singing finches and paired with the European goldfinch to produce a beautifully colored hybrid with an unusual song. Canaries have also been crossed with the red-hooded siskin to produce red-factor canaries. *An import, the red-hooded siskin is on the Endangered Species List.* It is illegal to buy one.

TABLE IV

Other Common Birds

DIAMOND DOVE (*Geopelia cuneata*)

Origin: Australia.

Availability: Commonly bred.

Nature: Tender, gentle, peaceable pets as individuals or in an aviary. They are loving to their offspring and to each other. They are floundering, bungling, careless birds. Even tiny finches and waxbills are safe in the same aviary with diamond doves. Don't put two breeding pairs together; they will fight.

Size: 7½ inches.

Song: A cooing accompanied by a raising and lowering of the head and fanning of the tail.

Color: Gray with a large pink circle around the eyes.

Cost: Inexpensive.

Diet: Millet, or finch or budgie mixture.

Breeding: Doves nest in almost anything, but like a canary nest or a somewhat deep dish of about five inches filled with hay or grasses. Some build their own nest— poorly—with twigs and grasses. Usually two eggs are laid and hatch in 11 days (though it may take 12 or 13 days). The young are supposed to be a cock and a hen, but the rule doesn't always hold true. You may need to remove all nests and nesting material to encourage the parents to feed the young until they are self-feeding. Otherwise the parents nest again too soon and may neglect their young.

Sexing: Young are almost impossible to sex. Adult cock has a darker eye ring then the hen and does a courting dance.

RINGNECK DOVE (*Streptopelia capicola*)
Origin: India.
Availability: Less common than diamond dove in some parts of the country, more popular in other localities.
Nature: A hearty, quiet bird that lives peaceably even with others of its own species. It has been domesticated for years. The white dove is a variation and is similar in nature.
Size: 9 inches. (Although large for a caged bird, they are so inactive they can live in relatively small quarters.)
Color: Fawn with a black band almost circling the neck.
Cost: Inexpensive.
Diet: Millet or budgie mix, although they will eat almost any grain.
Sexing: Difficult, females slightly smaller than males.

BUTTON QUAIL (*Turnix lepurana*)
Origin: Southeast Asia or Africa.
Availability: In some areas easy to find; in others difficult.
Nature: A most humorous bird who waddles, scrambles, and stands on its tiptoes to yell.
Size: 4 inches, a round little ball.
Song: Crows and makes a croaking sound a bit like a frog as its throat swells.
Color: Brown body, black face with a white slice under its chin. Hen is mostly brown and rather nondescript.
Cost: If you find them, they are inexpensive.
Diet: Chicken mash (chicken starter), ground Gaines or Purina Dog Chow, finch seed, greens, a bit of fruit, eggshells, canary grit, mealworms.

Breeding: The hen will nest under bushes, plastic greens, or a mound of hay in an overturned flowerpot or other container where she can gather her eggs. She needs grasses or hay placed close to her after she begins sitting, because she often won't weave a nest until she has her eggs together. Incubation period is 18 days. Limit clutch to 6 eggs. In a confined area remove the cock before the young hatch or he will kill them. Only young raised in an incubator will become tame.

PEACH-FACED LOVEBIRD (*Agapornis roseicollis*)
Origin: Africa.
Availability: In most states.
Nature: Scrappy and sassy; more lovable if hand-reared, but even these birds may start to nip and cannot be handled. There is no chance of taming one that has not been hand-fed as a nestling. Active and comical in a cage.
Size: 5½ to 6 inches.
Song: Chatter; they do not talk.
Life span: About 20 years.
Minimum size cage: Budgerigar.
Diet: Budgie mixture, plus some safflower or sunflower seeds, a few nuts, greens, fruits, vegetables, water, cuttlebone, mineral block. They love to chew wood and should have tree limbs to eat.
Note: There are other forms of lovebirds available, but this one is the most common in the United States.

A Free Pet You Can Tame

STARLING (*Sturnus vulgaris*)
Origin: U.S. These pests among birds may be taken from a nest outdoors and hand-fed.

Nature: A devoted pet; it will follow you around the house, greet you, sit on your shoulder. It is a thief by nature, so keep glittering objects you value out of sight.

Song: It has a raspy voice that can be irritating, but it can mimic a few words.

Diet: Omnivorous (it eats anything). Raise it on baby cereal to which you add a bit of ground beef. You may blend in some cooked, mashed carrot. It may also eat whole wheat bread soaked in warm milk.

Note: Starlings are one of the few native species it is legal to keep in captivity.

TABLE V

Parrots

The term parrot includes a large number of families and parrot-like birds. Parrots are more intelligent than smaller birds. Many species have the ability to imitate the human voice, which has made them popular through the centuries. But the parrot's personality, its lively reaction to humans, and its devotion to its owner make it especially popular today. Parrots also have an excessive curiosity, which leads them into the oddest situations and often makes them the clowns among birds.

Parrots may like a person immediately, but they can also take an intense dislike to someone. If you are a quiet, gentle person who is good with birds, if you are in your teens or older, you might win a parrot's heart. Its heart must be won for it to become either tame or a pleasant pet.

Cost: Expensive. The Amazon parrots and conurine parakeets are the most common and least expensive.

Size of cage: At least 6 inches wider than the width of

the bird with its wings outstretched. Heavy-duty metal
bars a parrot cannot bite in two.

Diet: Varies with the species. Buy a complete nutritional
diet for parrots. Mixes are sold for small parrots, parakeets, and large parrots. Lories eat a diet for soft-billed
birds. Parrot mix includes oats, wheat hearts, sunflower
(sometimes safflower) seeds, large millet, canary seed,
nuts. Also feed greens, fruits and vegetables, grasses,
mineral block. Tree limbs to chew are a must. Some
varieties of parrots need thistle.

Note: Parrots that come out of quarantine should be fed
two tablespoons of buttermilk, yogurt, sour milk, or sour
cream in their water the first few days (to offset the
medication they were given in quarantine). Otherwise
they cannot digest their food.

Parrot-type Birds That Are Generally Considered Good Pets

Scientifically, the order of Parrots is divided into many
categories of different types of birds. The order of Parrots is called by the technical name Psittaciformes. The
family name is Psittacidae. All psittacines, which have
been called here hook-billed birds, belong to this family.
Three of the subfamilies are well known to those who
keep psittacines for pets: one includes lories and lorikeets,
another cockatoos, and the third macaws, conures, parrots, and parakeets. Each of these has its own grouping
of one or more genera. Technically, a parakeet, or macaw,
or cockatoo is not the same as a parrot, although they are
all part of the large group—the Parrot family.

AMAZON PARROTS

There are about fifty species of Amazon parrots. They
are natives of Central and South America, hence have

become popular in the United States, which is close to their native lands. Some Amazons are quite small, some large. The general overall color of most of them is green, but they have distinguishing bright colors such as red, blue, and yellow in patches on their heads, wings, and tails. Most of them have the ability to learn to talk. Amazons as a group are felt to be less noisy than other parrots.

THE AFRICAN GRAY (*Psittacus erithacus erithacus*)
Best known for its talking ability, usually thought to top the list in this category. If it is trained by hand-feeding as a nestling, it can make an excellent pet. Otherwise it is likely to be noisy, high-strung, and nasty. It is an expensive bird.

CONURINE PARAKEETS
This group of birds is often called "bee bee parrots," after a small six and a half inch bird by this name. The group includes species such as the canary-winged, white-winged, orange-(bronze-)winged, and tui parakeets. The Bee Bee Parakeet (*Brotogeris jugularis*) is recommended most often of the birds in this group. It is docile, relatively easy to tame, and might learn to speak a few words. Conurine parakeets are easier to feed and make better pets than conures.

RED-RUMPED PARAKEET (*Psephotus haematonotus*)
The size of a cockatiel. It cannot learn to talk, but will whistle prettily. It is not as likely to be a screecher as some parrots are. It has a life span of about twenty years. Many people in the United States have been breeding this parakeet for some time, so it is possible to find one that has been hand-fed as a nestling if you read the ads in bird magazines.

MACAWS

These are expensive, colorful, large birds. All except the scarlet macaw (which is stubborn and vicious) have the potential to be good pets.

COCKATOOS

An intelligent, affectionate bird for a pet, provided they are hand-fed as nestlings. The demand for them has fostered a great deal of smuggling. Cockatoos are large birds with powerful jaws. Avoid the lesser sulphurcrested cockatoo, for it has a wild nature and will not be a good pet.

The macaws and cockatoos listed here are only to give a complete list of the parrots and parrot-like birds recommended for pets. They are large and expensive, so that only a few young people would be able to handle one or to afford one. It should also be noted that individual birds in almost any species sometimes become loving pets because of specialized training; no one can rule out a species of birds any more than a class of people as all good or all bad. Rare species should not be kept as pets, but used for breeding in an effort to increase their numbers for future generations.

TABLE VI

Uncommon Birds: Soft-billed Birds

Diet: Nectar, fruits and cooked vegetables, greens, cucumber, moistened high-protein dog food, insectivorous mixture, mealworms or other live food, eggs. Do not feed seed.

PEKIN ROBIN (sometimes called Pekin nightingale or Japanese robin) (*Leiothrix lutea*)

Origin: India and Hong Kong.

Availability: In areas where it it bred it is not difficult to find one; otherwise rare. (They have been liberated in Hawaii and thrive in the wild there.)

Nature: A swift-flying, intelligent bird. A bouncing, bounding, teasing clown.

Size: About 7 inches; a plump bird.

Song: A loud, clear, cheery, warm-throated warble.

Color: Basic color is olive, but what you see is the bright yellow orange on the face and throat.

Cost: Ranges with finches at the higher end of the scale.

Sociability: Compatible with other birds in an aviary. May even buddy up with a fledgling from another species.

Diet: Listed above. May eat some finch seed, which is unusual in a soft-billed bird. It will keep a house clean of spiders and roaches if it flies free.

Note: Flying room necessary because it loses its feathers if it is confined to a small cage.

LORIES

Parrot-like birds sold as parrots, which are listed here because they eat the same diet as the one listed above. Lorries are beautiful, often clever, but generally unfriendly. A soft diet of fruits means soft droppings; because of a lory's size, they squirt all over the cage and room. The diet is time-consuming to prepare and must be changed frequently. Not recommended as a pet for an amateur.

APPENDIX II

CONSTRUCTING A SIMPLE AVIARY

Hardware Cloth

Materials: Hardware cloth with ¼ inch mesh for finches; ½ inch mesh for canaries and budgies. Cookie sheet for the bottom. Spring clothespin. Tin snips.

Construction: Bend the hardware cloth into a rectangular box. With tin snips cut a 5-inch square opening in the front of "cage." Also cut a 7-inch square of hardware cloth to overlap your door opening. Hang it from the top with wire loops you make. Lock it with the spring clothespin. All cut edges should be folded out to prevent the bird from rubbing against them.

Converted Bookcase

Materials: Unfinished bookcase, preferably with no back and removable shelves. (Any bookcase may be used, but if painted, sand it clean.) A piece of hardware cloth large enough to cover the back as far down as the top of the lowest shelf. A piece of hardware cloth (or heavy-duty plastic) the same size. A piece of plywood large enough to cover back below hardware cloth. Tacks. Tin snips. Optional: fluorescent light; unleaded white paint.

Construction: Tack the bottom shelf in place. Tack the plywood on the back between the bottom shelf and the bottom of the bookcase. (This is your storage section and also gives stability to the bookcase.)

In one piece of wire mesh cut a door near the middle the same way as described in Hardware Cloth aviary. Tack both pieces of wire mesh onto the bookcase. Leave a ¼-inch opening between the top of the bottom shelf and the lower edge of one piece of hardware cloth (so newspapers may be slid in and out for the bottom of the aviary).

If old bookcase is used: remove the back except for the section behind the bottom shelf. Cover the space with hardware cloth to make the aviary light. Tack hardware cloth on the front, as above. If the bookcase is to be placed against the wall, do not use the mesh on the back —it would not serve a purpose.

Paint the bookcase with unleaded white paint. Mount the light.

The Basic Aviary
STEP-BY-STEP DIRECTIONS
by Michael Shays

If you had a horse, you would want to build a corral around him so he could move about without wandering into trouble. A bird needs a special kind of corral, one with fencing at the top as well as the sides so that he won't fly into trouble. You might call his corral a cage, but it's really his home, complete with his own backyard to play in, where he can feel safe and comfortable. Some birds need cages to keep them in. Others need cages to keep people and cats out. Whatever the reason your bird needs a cage, the bigger the better. Large cages give him the chance to exercise his wings and enjoy the freedom of flight. Large cages also give several nesting pairs the privacy they need.

You can build a flight cage yourself with just a yardstick, some tin snips, and a hammer (and a staple gun if you have had experience using one) if you can get all the pieces precut at the lumber company. Here is what you should ask your lumber dealer to cut for you:

1. Four 2″ x 2″ pieces of framing lumber, each exactly 6 feet long. These are for the legs.

2. Four 1″ x 2″ pieces of framing lumber, each 21½ inches long. These are for the left and right sides of the cage.

3. Four 2″ x 2″ pieces of framing lumber, each 40 inches long. These are for the front and back sides of the cage.

4. Two 2″ x 2″ pieces of framing lumber, each 21½ inches long. These are for the top or ceiling of the cage.

5. One piece of AC exterior plywood ⅜″ or ½″ thick, cut 37 inches long and 24 inches wide. This is for the bottom of the cage.

When you buy the framing lumber, you may wish to substitute clear pine, which is better. However, spruce without too many knots is much less expensive and will do the job just as well. Don't be concerned when the 2″ x 2″ measures 1½″ x 1½″ (or even a little bit smaller if you buy clear pine) and the 1″ x 2″ measures ¾″ x

1½". They were the right sizes when they were cut into lumber, but they were made smaller when the lumber mill planed all the surfaces smooth. The important thing is to make sure your lumber dealer cuts all the lengths the right size.

There are a few other things you have to get for the cage besides lumber. These are:

6. One piece of ½" mesh hardware cloth cut 24 inches wide and exactly eleven *feet* long. This is for the left and right sides and top of the cage.

7. About one hundred wire staples to hold the hardware cloth in place.

8. About forty 2" ringed-type flathead nails, and about thirty 2½" ringed-type flathead nails to hold the framing lumber together. Boxnails can also be used instead of the ringed-type, but they don't hold as well. For a very solid construction use 2½" number 8 or 20 flathead screws instead of the longer ringed nails.

9. One green plastic "Astroturf" type doormat, measuring 21½" x 35½". This will be the floor of your cage.

10. A small bottle of white-type wood glue.

11. A set of four chrome or nylon table-leg glides.

12. A quart of white enamel lead-free paint or one of the new white plastic varnishes.

13. Four sheets of ¼" plate glass measuring 20 inches wide and 43¾ inches high. These are for the front and back of the cage and are the most expensive pieces to buy. You can substitute less expensive materials for the back if you want to keep the cost of your cage down.

The most practical substitute would be a single sheet of ⅜″ or ½″ AC plywood, cut 40 inches wide and 48 inches high. If you do this, eliminate two of the pieces of framing lumber in Item 3 above. The advantage is less cost and greater cage strength. The disadvantage of this substitute is that you will no longer be able to see *through* the cage or be able to view it from all four sides. But if you will always have the cage up against a solid opaque wall, there really is no reason to spend the extra for a glass back. Be sure to buy extra nails if you get a plywood back.

Another substitute would be to cover the back with a 40″ x 48″ sheet of hardware cloth, but this has the disadvantage over glass of allowing seed and feathers to fly into the room as well as reducing visibility. If the aviary is to be set against a wall, you can make a solid back if you prefer. You may also substitute plexiglass or wire mesh for the front. The mesh should be ½ inch by 4 inches if you can find it, or else ½ inch by 2 inches or ½ inch by 1 inch. When sprayed with a flat, non-toxic black paint, the birds will be quite visible. Be sure to buy extra staples if you get a screen back.

When you purchase the glass for the front (and also if you decide to use glass for the back as well), ask you glass dealer to cut it for a double roller track for openings 39½ inches wide and 45 inches high. Two panels each will be needed for the front and back and will overlap about ½ inch in the center. He will give you the exact measurements for the double track he sells, will polish the edges of the glass so they won't cut, will mount the bottom edges (the 20 inch ends) of the glass in a metal strip with rollers, and supply top and bottom tracks 39½ inches long for the back and front panels to ride in. If he has a lighter weight glass that can be mounted in a double deck, this is worth the slightly extra cost.

14. If you use glass for both the front and back sides, it is also a good precaution to buy a set of four 4″ corner irons. In this case you will also need to add a screwdriver and pilot hole drill to your tool kit.

Once you have assembled all the parts to your flight cage, lay everything except the glass on the floor or on a work table in the order that they are listed above. Everything there? Okay, let's put it together.

BUILDING THE AVIARY

First, read all the instructions to the end so that you get a general idea of what is coming next. This will help keep you from making a mistake because the instructions weren't clear.

15. Take that long roll of hardware cloth (Item 6) and lay it out flat on the floor. If it wants to roll back up, turn it upside down and put something heavy like a book on each end. Take your yardstick and hold it along one of the short ends. It should measure 24 inches. Now mark off 1½ inches along this left side (the long edge) until you have cut 48 inches (four feet) off the edge of the cloth. You can cut the thin piece off and throw it away.

Go back to the same end where you started cutting and measure 1½ inches from the *right* side. Cut along this opposite long edge until you have cut

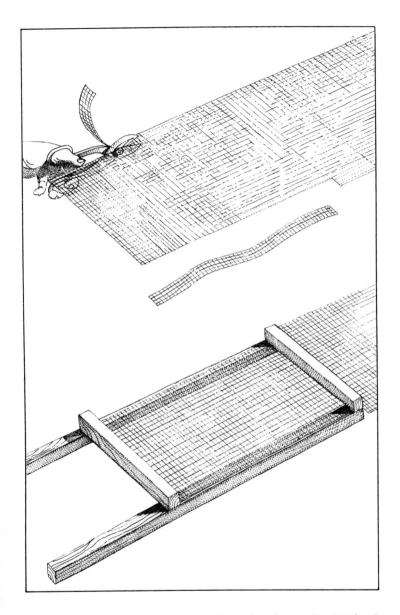

Building an aviary: steps 15 to 20 in the design by Michael Shays

48 inches along this edge. You can cut off this thin piece and throw it away. Check the short end now. It should measure 21 inches.

Repeat these same steps with the other short end. When you have finished, the hardware cloth will be 21 inches wide for four feet at either end, and 24 inches wide for the center three feet.

16. Take the four legs (Item 1) and see that they measure exactly 72 inches. Place them *under* the hardware cloth along the side edges you just cut away, leaving 24½ inches extending out beyond the narrow end of the cloth. When you have done this with all four of the legs, it will look like a first aid stretcher with 24½ inch "handles." Of course, there will be no side rails where the hardware cloth is wider, because the legs don't come together in the middle.

Now line up any one of the legs so that the cloth covers all but ¼ inch of the side of one of the legs. (Be sure to keep the "handle" 24½ inches long.) This is so the sharp ends of the cloth won't stick out and snag you when you are tending the cage. Nail the cloth to the leg with a staple about every three inches.

Do the same thing to the leg on the opposite (parallel) side of the cloth. You now have the legs of one side of the cage fastened to the hardware cloth.

17. Now check to make sure that the space between the two legs which are fastened and those which are not is exactly 37 inches. It is more important that this distance be 37 inches than that the "handles" on the last two legs are 24½ inches. Line these

legs up so all but ¼ inch is covered by the cloth, and fasten them to the cloth with staples.

The finished product will still look like a stretcher with 37 inches of rail missing in the center.

18. Measure exactly 24 inches from the end of each of the "handles" and make a mark with a sharp pencil. Now take two of the short pieces of 1" x 2" (Item 2) and place them *on top of* the cloth at the marks, going from one leg across to the other parallel one. The pieces should rest *above* your mark, leaving 24 inches of "handle" below. You may have to stretch the cloth a bit at this point to make sure the cross-pieces are square at each corner. When this is done, nail them to the legs with two of the shorter ringed nails at each joint. Do this for the crosspiece at each end of the hardware cloth.

19. Now get the other two short pieces of 1" x 2" (Item 2) and lay them *on top of* the cloth from the top of one leg across to the top of the parallel leg. These two pieces should be exactly 37 inches apart. Make sure they are square at each corner and nail them to the legs with the shorter ringed nails.

20. Turn the hardware cloth over and fasten the cloth to the four crossbars with staples. Be sure that all corners are square before you hammer in the staples.

21. Now lift the legs up from the *center* of the hardware cloth so that the cloth makes an arch over you. You will need someone tall to help you with this step. With your hammer tap down the hardware cloth so that it bends over the edges of the top crosspieces at a right angle. In order to do this the legs must be on the outside of the cloth and the crosspieces must be inside.

22. You now have the left side, the top, and the right side of the cage formed. Place it gently in this shape on what will be the back of the cage. So that you don't bend the wide part of the hardware cloth, slip one of the 40-inch pieces of 2″ x 2″ (Item 3) under the top part of the two back legs.

Take another one of the 40-inch pieces (from Item 3) and place it across the two front legs. Slide it all the way up to the top, up snugly against but still under the wide part of the hardware cloth. The ends of this piece should line up with the outside edges of the legs. You may have to pull the hardware cloth tight to see this. Make sure each corner is square, squeeze some glue where the pieces fit, and nail this piece to the top of the legs with two of the longer ringed nails at each joint. For a stronger joint use screws instead of nails.

23. If you are going to have a glass or hardware cloth back, turn the cage over on its front and nail the other 40-inch piece of 2″ x 2″ across the top of the back as you did for the front. Again, use screws for a stronger joint.

If you are going to have a plywood back, nail the piece of plywood to the back at this time with the good side facing in. Be sure to line up the outside edges of the plywood with the outside edges of the legs so that the back of the cage has four square corners. Bend the excess hardware cloth at the top over the plywood with your hammer and fasten it to the back with staples.

24. Turn the cage on its back again and measure down each front leg from the bottom of the top crosspiece exactly 45 inches. Make a mark with a sharp pencil

and place another 40-inch piece of 2″ x 2″ across the legs just below your marks so that you have a 45-inch opening between the upper and lower crosspieces. Make sure all corners are square. Glue and nail or glue and use screws.

25. If you are going to have a glass or hardware cloth back, turn the cage over and repeat Step 24 for the back.

26. Turn the cage *upside down*. Place the plywood floor (Item 5) with the good side down (facing into the cage) on the bottom four crosspieces. (This will form a little well inside the cage when you turn it back up.) It should come up snug between the legs at the left and right sides, but will be about ½ inch smaller front to back. Remove the plywood, apply glue along the crosspieces, replace the plywood (good side down), center, and nail in place with the shorter ringed nails.

27. If you are going to have a glass back, at this point you may want to strengthen the frame by installing corner irons under the flooring. Place them against the front and back legs running left and right along the long edge of the plywood floor. Support is not needed going front to back.

28. Leave the cage upside down. Take the two short pieces of 2″ x 2″ (Item 4) and place them inside the ceiling of the cage from the front crosspiece across to the back. Arrange them so that they are about 12 inches from the side crosspieces and from each other. Push them up snugly against the hardware cloth, make sure they are square, and fasten them with the longer ringed nails from the front and back. There is little extra advantage in using screws here.

29. Nail the upper track for the glass panels into the front upper crosspiece, using nails supplied by the glass dealer. If you are going to have glass at the back, nail the upper track for those panels into the rear upper crosspiece.

30. Nail the chrome or nylon table leg glides into each of the cage legs.

31. If you are going to have a hardware cloth back, place the cage face down on the front and fasten the cloth with staples at this time. Be sure all corners are square before you begin.

32. Stand the cage on its legs. Nail the lower tracks for the glass panels on top of the lower front and back crosspieces. Be sure to align the lower track directly under the upper track or the glass panels will lean in or out.

33. Fasten the top of the hardware cloth to the front and back crosspieces and the two ceiling supports with staples.

34. If you want to paint your cage, use a finish with an easy-to-clean surface which has no lead.

35. Install the "Astroturf" flooring. It should just fit, but it can be trimmed if it doesn't.

36. Install the glass panels, one in the inside track and the other in the outside track, by inserting the top end of the panel into the upper track first.

37. You might want to cut a service door in the mesh at one end of the aviary. Cut it in the way described for the hardware cloth cage at the beginning of this section.

There's your cage. It has a floor, walls, and a ceiling. From here on it's up to your own imagination and ingenuity. You can clip off a small dogwood branch and hang

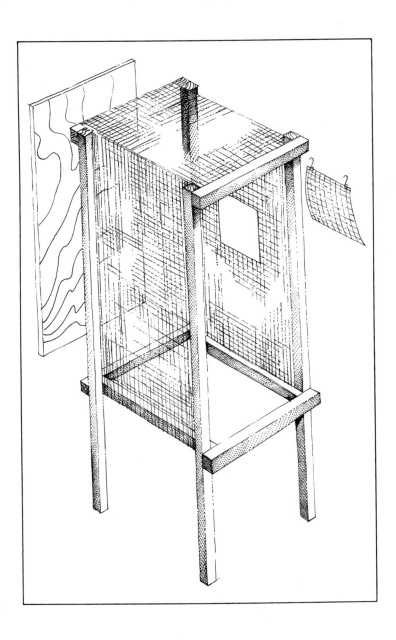

A nearly completed homemade aviary

it from the ceiling for perches that look natural. You can hang houses and feeders from the ceiling or tie them to one of the sides. You can place a lamp at the sides for heat, or you can put a fixture directly on the top of the hardware cloth for light. If it is right over a high perch, it will even give heat, unless of course it is a fluorescent type fixture. If it won't make the cage top-heavy, you can even put a hanging plant or vine on the top of the cage to soften the corners. Do not put a grow light for plants on top of the cage, however, as it will harm the birds. A special Vita-Lite made by Durolite especially for birds may be used.

Some day you can even join two or more cages together by cutting an opening for a flight tunnel in one of the sides.

OUTDOOR AVIARY

Framing: 2 x 4's. Make your first one small. Nail hardware cloth or metal netting to the inside of the frame and the roof. Extend it *below* the ground for at least a foot, then bend it outward for another foot or two. (Mice dig close to a fence, bump the mesh and give up.) House screen may be nailed to the *outside* of the 2 x 4's to form a buffer against cats, mosquitoes, snakes, and baby mice but it tends to obscure your view of the birds. A metal or cement curb 18 inches high around the outside of the fence also discourages mice and snakes. Drape netting on the roof, secure it tightly around all the edges. (Cats— who love to leap on aviary roofs—dislike the swaying footing of the net.)

An old toolshed, a section of a porch or a garage, or part of a basement where a window opens may serve as the shelter portion of an outdoor aviary. Part of the aviary itself may be enclosed with siding or heavy plastic firmly fastened against winds. A shelter is necessary. Birds roost there at night and retreat into it in storms. Keep food dishes inside it. Face it so the wind and rain from storms do not swamp the inside. Be sure it is draft-free.

Use double doors on a vestibule or enter from inside a building so birds cannot escape to the great outdoors. A low door, just high enough to stoop through, helps prevent escapes because birds tend to fly high when they are startled.

Floors of cement hose down easily. Hard-packed dirt or a planted aviary may be used. Some chicken farmers eliminate odor with a compost flooring. Line the bottom of a 3½-foot-deep pit with crushed stone for drainage. Cover the stone with a layer of soil, then some good compost and well-rotted manure. The active soil organisms in the rotted manure and compost feed on the fresh droppings. There's no odor. Twice a year clean out the pit; the droppings can be used immediately for fertilizer.

A Cage or an Aviary for a Cockatiel
Designed by Johonet Wicks

MATERIALS

1. 2 circular trays with the edges raised 2 inches. Diameter: 30 inches. Have the trays cut by a sheet metal company. They should be creased through the center for extra strength. Have four holes drilled an equal distance apart in the raised sides of the metal trays.
2. A roll of heavy-duty wire mesh 3 feet by 8 feet 1 inch. Openings in the mesh should be 1 by 2 inches.
3. Picture wire for fastening the mesh.
4. 4 pieces of hardwood for legs: 1½ inches x 1½ inches x four feet.
5. 8 2″ bolts with smooth, rounded ends. 8 nuts to fit the bolts.

CONSTRUCTION

Tip the metal trays on their edges three feet apart with the raised edges facing inward. Line up the holes drilled in the edges. The trays form the top and bottom of the cage. Roll the wire mesh around the outside of the trays, keeping it flush with the top and bottom edges of the cage. Stretch the mesh tight as you roll it. It should overlap. Wire the edges of the wire mesh together. Wire them tightly so no holes are left through which the cockatiel can slip a toenail. To attach the legs: drill two holes in each piece of hardwood, one at the top, one three feet away. Be sure the two holes line up with the holes drilled in the raised edges on the metal trays. Insert the bolts through the holes in the trays and into the holes in the hardwood legs. The rounded ends of the bolts should be *inside* the cage. Cut a five-inch door in the middle of the wire mesh and an overlapping seven-inch square of mesh to cover it. Hang the door at the top with wire loops. Secure it with a wire clip.

APPENDIX III

FEEDING

This list includes foods fed by breeders and bird experts in this country. It would be difficult to catalogue all such foods, but these are mentioned the most frequently.

GREENS

Easy to find: Romaine lettuce, spinach, broccoli, Brussels sprouts, tops of vegetables.

Ones breeders mention most often: Collards, kale, comfrey, endive, rape, spinach.

Easy to find in the wild: Dandelion, clover, chickweed, grass (rye, lawn clippings, etc.) Caution: wash wild greens, too.

Others: Endive, escarole, watercress, chard, mustard, kelp, alfalfa (fresh or dried), chicory, comfrey, nasturtiums.

Do not feed: Parsley (it can be poisonous to birds), iceberg lettuce, celery, cabbage.

SEEDING GRASSES

May be in the milky, blade or ripe stage. Easy ones to grow at home include bird seed mixture, millet, chickweed, alfalfa, lettuce—feed when 2 to 4 inches high.

SEEDS

Flax, oats, poppy (maw), niger (thistle), sunflower, safflower, pumpkin, sesame, lettuce, celery, carrot, foxtail, anise, "gold of pleasure," teazle, plantain, clover, linseed, cabbage, green or ornamental pepper, rape, millet, corn, wheat. (Many of above are found in treat mixtures.) Packages of garden seeds (lettuce, strawberry, radish, small flowers, etc.)

BASIC SEED MIXTURES

Canary: Rape, canary seed.

Budgie: White (proso) millet, canary seed, oats.

Finch: Yellow millet (panicum, often called finch seed), red millet, white millet, canary.

Cockatiel: Large white (proso) millet, canary, oats, sunflower.

Parakeet: Same as cockatiel, who is a parakeet; some mixtures contain paddy rice, buckwheat, safflower.

Parrot: Large millet, canary, sunflower, safflower, oats, wheat hearts, nuts; may also include corn. Different size parrots have different mixtures. Buy a mix prepared for your species.

VEGETABLES

Raw: Carrots (grated, chopped, strips), spinach, broccoli, Brussels sprouts, corn, peas, beans, zucchini, tomatoes, cucumber, seeds of green peppers.

Frozen: Mixed vegetables, peas, etc. (after thawing).

Cooked: Broccoli, Brussels sprouts, spinach, corn, peas, squash (the yellower the better), yams, sweet potatoes, white potatoes.

FRUITS

Easy to find: Oranges, apples, bananas.

Berries: Blueberry, raspberry, blackberry, strawberry, currant, pyracantha.

Melons: Watermelon, Spanish, honeydew, cantaloupe, etc.

Others: Pears, figs, plums, peaches, cherries, apricots, pineapple, nuts (such as raw peanuts, walnuts), raisins, canned fruit.

Do not feed: Avocado (it is poisonous to birds). Some wild berries are poisonous; only feed ones you know.

TREE LIMBS

Fruit trees (apple, pear, cherry, etc.), nut, hardwoods (maple, oak, etc.), honeysuckle, forsythia, willow, dogwood, relatives of eucalyptus.

SOME HIGH-PROTEIN FOODS

Eggs (scrambled, hard-boiled), raw ground beef, mealworms, fruit flies, live bugs, peanut butter, bananas, milk (whole, powdered), dog food, currants, raisins.

SOFT-BILLED BIRDS' FOODS (lories, mynahs, etc.)

Fruit (fresh, frozen, canned), honey, insectile mixture, soybean meal, game starter, baby food, milk, cottage cheese, whole wheat bread, and high-protein foods listed above.

OIL

Wheat germ oil (for vitamin E), cod liver oil (vitamins A, D); both are necessary when oil is used. Oils should be refined for human rather than animal use.

VITAMINS

One drop every other day in 4 ounces of water (the size of a bird's drinking cup). Never overfeed vitamins because they can kill a bird. Measure accurately.

Recipe for Soaked Seed

Method used to retain food value in spite of soaking. Invert a nine-inch glass or Pyrex pie tin into a twelve-inch one. Cover the top dish with a square piece of burlap or other rough cloth so the four corners hang into the bottom dish. Fill the bottom dish half full of water. The burlap acts as a blotter to absorb the water through the dangling corners. Scatter seeds on top of the burlap. When they swell and become soft, they are ready to be fed to the bird. Since they spoil quickly, do not leave them more than two hours in a cage. (Sprouted seeds may be stored in the refrigerator in a plastic bag.)

Vitamins and Proteins

Seeds	Vitamin A	Vitamin B complex	Vitamin C	Vitamin E	Protein
canary	x	x			x
rape	x	x		x	x
oats	x	x			x
flax	x	x			x
poppy	x	x		x	x
niger	x	x	x	x	x
sunflower	x	x		x	x
pumpkin	x	x			x
sesame		x			x

OTHER SOURCES FOR:

vitamin A: Green or yellow vegetable matter, mealworms.

vitamin B complex: Mealworms, dessicated liver, cornmeal, yeast, egg yolk, some vegetables.

vitamin C: Vegetation, rosehips, orange, grapefruit, apple, mealworms, cod liver oil.

vitamin D: Vegetables and fruit, cod liver oil. (Birds exposed to the sun get enough; ones in places such as a basement need cod liver oil year round.)

vitamin E: Wheat germ oil (contains a lot), vegetation.

SOURCES FOR:

minerals: Sunflower, safflower, vegetables, mealworms, eggshells.

natural oils: Niger, flax, seeds from green peppers, peanut butter.

high-protein seeds: Niger, maw.

high in carbohydrates: Millet, canary, linseed, niger, maw.

APPENDIX IV

HOW TO FIND IT

Look at the ads in bird magazines first:

The AFA Watchbird, American Federation of Aviculture, 443 W. Douglas Ave., El Cajon, CA 92020. (Hereafter referred to as AFA).

American Cage Bird Magazine, 3449 N. Western Ave., Chicago, IL 60618. (Hereafter referred to as ACBM).

Bird World: American Aviculturists' Gazette, Box 70, North Hollywood, CA 91601 (Hereafter referred to as BW).

Audubon Society: see National Audubon.

Aviaries, indoor
   Phillips, Mrs. Wendell C., Jr., "Building an Attractive Indoor Aviary," *ACBM*, Dec. 1972, 17.

Aviaries, outdoor
   Clymire, T. George, "Aviary for the Novice," *AFA*, Aug./Sept. 1978, 12.

Klingler, Kenneth P., "Wintering in Outside Aviaries,"
ACBM, Nov. 1977, 35.
Breeding
Rogers, Cyril H., "Birds That Can Be Bred in Cap-
tivity," *Encyclopedia of Cage and Aviary Birds*
(N.Y.: Macmillan Publishing Co., 1975).

Endangered species
Current issues of *ACBM* and *AFA* (list new birds which
have been added).
Endangered Species List (including birds), U.S. Department of the Interior, Bureau of Sport Fisheries
and Wildlife, Washington, DC 20240.

Feeder for wild birds and aviaries
E-Z FIL Feeder by Plastico, P.O. Box 2, Camden, OH
45311.

Food sources for vitamins and minerals
Hart, Ernest H., *Budgerigar Handbook*, (Neptune
City, NJ: T.F.H. Publications, 1970), 110-111.

Germinating seeds
Kranz, Frederick H. and Jacqueline L., *Gardening In-
doors Under Lights* (N.Y.: Viking Press, 1971), 122.
Runnals, Mark, "Raising Your Own Seed," *ACBM*,
Oct. 1975, 26.

Importing birds with you when you return from abroad
Checklist of birds allowed as imports and forms to fill
out to travel into the U.S. with a bird: Chief Staff
Veterinarian Services, Dept. of Agriculture, Federal
Building, Hyattsville, MD 20782.
"How to Import Pets Not Disease," Department of
Health, Education and Welfare, Public Health Serv-
ice, Center for Disease Control, Atlanta, GA 30333.

"USDA's New Bird Cage Is a Lifesaver," *AFA*, Oct./ Nov. 1979, 19.

Lights for cages and aviaries—pamphlet
   Pet and Aquarium Lighting, Duro-Lite Lamps, Inc., 17-10 Willow St., Fair Lawn, NJ 17410. Request form DL-315. Enclose a self-addressed, stamped envelop.
   Kranz, Frederick H. and Jacqueline L., (see above) has a chapter on balanced lighting.

Light, how much artificial light?
   Wahlin, William S., Ph.D., "Light . . . and the Breeding of Birds," *ACBM*, Sept. 1977, 28. (Includes latitude table and daylight hours.)

Mealworms, how to raise them
   Roots, Clive, *Soft-billed Birds*, (N.Y.: Arco Publishing Co., 1970), 58.

Minerals and vitamins in foods birds eat
   Hart, Ernest H., *Budgerigar Handbook*, (Neptune City, NJ: T.F.H. Publications, 1970), 110-111.
National Audubon Society: 950 Third Avenue, New York, N.Y. 10022.

Petamine and Budgimine
   Most suppliers distribute them; many pet shops sell them.
   Write Kellogg Seed Co., 322 E. Florida St., Milwaukee, WI 53201 for distributor nearest you.

Poisonous plants in U.S.
   Bulletin IB 104, Mailing Room, 7 Research Park, Cornell University, Ithaca, NY 14853. Inquire for price; it is inexpensive, under a dollar.

Recipes for hand-feeding nestlings and sick birds
Hall, Jo, *Cockatiels . . . Care and Breeding*, (Austin, Texas: Sweet Publishing Co., 1976), pp. 21, 32.

Recipes for insectile mixture for soft-billed birds
Roots, Clive, *Soft-billed Birds*, (NY: Arco Publishing Co., 1970).
Roots, Clive, "Feeding the Soft-bills," *ACBM*, Oct. 1972, 7.

Sterilizing soil for an aviary or cage
Kranz, Frederick H. and Jacqueline L., *Gardening Indoors Under Lights*, (NY: Viking Press, 1971), 90.

Societies
American Budgerigar Society, Inc., Elizabeth M. Tefft, 2 Farnum Rd., Warwick, RI 02888.
American Cockatiel Society, 9812 Bois D'Arc Court, Ft. Worth, TX 76126.
Cooperative Canary Breeders' Association, Miss Jane Scott, 3659 Edenhurst Ave., Los Angeles, CA 90039.
The Zebra Finch Society of America, David W. Seabury, 8204 Woodland Ave., Annandale, VA 22003.

GLOSSARY OF TERMS COMMONLY APPLIED TO BIRDS

acclimatize to adjust to a new climate or different environment.

albino a mutation in which all the dark coloring is missing, leaving only white. Eyes are red; feet and legs, pink.

aviary a room or large cage where birds fly free.

aviculture the hobby of keeping birds.

aviculturist someone who raises or cares for birds.

budgerigar a species of grass parakeet. "Budgie" for short.

candle (eggs) viewing an egg with a light (originally with a candle) to see if it is fertile.

cere a fleshy piece without feathers across the top of the bill in some birds.

chromosomes carry the genes that have the hereditary characteristics.

clutch the eggs a hen lays to hatch at one time; the chicks who hatch from them.

cock male bird.

colony breeding a group of birds nesting in the same area.

color food a soft food to which a red coloring agent is added which enriches the natural color of certain birds.

crop a swelling in the digestive tube behind a bird's mouth.

cuttlebone bone from a cuttlefish.

domestically bred birds bred within the United States.

domesticated a species that has been bred in captivity for many generations.

droppings excrement of a bird.

egg-binding inability to expel an egg when the hen is laying.

endangered species birds (and all other flora and fauna) who are threatened with extinction in the wild. The list is kept by the United States Department of the Interior, Fish and Wildlife Service. A bird on this list is contraband. It cannot be imported or transported across state lines or owned without a permit. The international list is kept by the Convention on International Trade in Endangered Species of Wild Fauna and Flora.

Fancy a name used to describe certain types of breeds, especially canaries.

fledge to rear a bird until it is able to fly; able to fly.

fledgling a young bird who is just able to fly.

flight cage a large-size cage.

flight feathers the long wing feathers.

French molt a feather condition that affects the wings and tail, making them break off. No known cure. Sometimes an ailment in budgerigars.

gizzard the organ in which a bird's food is ground up.

gravel see grit.

greens leafy vegetables and other green-colored food such as lettuce, beet tops.

grit sandy type material used to digest food in gizzard.

ground color the basic color of white or yellow on which all other colors are superimposed.

hardware cloth wire mesh, a screening material.

hen female bird.

hybrid the result of a cross between any two species.

immature a bird who has not grown adult plumage (feathers with adult colors) and who is too young to breed.

inbreeding mating birds with close blood relationships.

incubate to set on and hatch eggs; to hatch eggs in an incubator.

insectivorous a bird who lives on insects and plants rather than seed.

leg band a narrow band slipped on a bird's leg when it is in the nest. As the foot grows, the band cannot slip off again, so he wears it for life. Initials on the band identify the bird's parentage to the breeder. The color of the band indicates the year of birth. Bands are issued by bird clubs and associations. Plastic bands may be put on at any age by any owner to distinguish or identify birds. Suppliers sell them. Nylon bands may be on birds that have been in import stations.

molting the process of shedding and replacing feathers.

nectivorous (nectarines) birds who live mainly on nectar from flowers.

nest to build a nest and raise young.

nestling a young bird still in the nest.

nestling food food that is fed to breeding hens and young; usually it is mixed with egg.

Newcastle a disease that can kill cage birds infected with it; it is associated with poultry; rare within the U.S.

niger thistle, a seed.

nontoxic nonpoisonous.

normal usually means the wild type of bird. Sometimes it describes the common color of a bird—gray zebra finches may be called normal zebra finches.

nuptial plumage breeding plumage; this is the spring dress of North American birds.

omnivorous birds who eat a wide variety of foods (both animal and vegetable).

ornithologist someone who studies birds.

ornithology a branch of zoology dealing with birds.

parakeet imprecise term for budgerigar, but widely used in the U.S. The name for a large family of birds which includes 115 species (one of which is the budgerigar).

pied a bird whose color is broken with light areas (colors are mixed).

pin feather a feather still encased that has not unfurled.

primaries the long flight feathers on a bird's wing (9-12 of them).

psittacine birds of the parrot family; hook-billed birds.

Red Factor the genetic factor bred into canaries by crossing a canary with the red-hooded siskin. The hybrids have colors from deep orange to almost red.

secondaries the shorter feathers on the wing (after the bend of the wing).

soft-bill birds which feed on insects and plants.

soft food blended mixtures of bread crumbs, crackers, or meal and other ingredients. Sometimes soft food means any food that is easy to digest and spoils easily.

species a classification for groups of mutually fertile birds (those birds who can mate only with other birds in the same group and whose young are fertile).

supplementary foods foods fed in addition to the basic seed diet.

suppliers   in this book, companies who sell bird food and equipment.

thistle   niger.

vent   the area between the back of a bird's legs and the top of the tail.

wild type   the form of the species found in the wild (outdoors in their native land).

young   baby birds, immature birds.

SUGGESTED READING

Ames, Felicia, *The Bird You Care For*, New York: Signet Books, 1970. A small, well-written book with basic instructions for bird care.

Bates, Henry J. and Busenbark, Robert I., *Finches and Soft-Billed Birds*, Neptune City, NJ: T.F.H. Publications, Inc., 1963.

————, *Parrots and Related Birds*, Neptune City, NJ: T.F.H. Publications, Inc., 1969. Basic reference work on parrots, parakeets, macaws, cockatoos, lories, etc. Also covers diet, aviaries, and other useful information on care of birds.

Baumhardt, L.H., "Budgie Talk," *American Cage Bird Magazine*, Jan. 1977, 13; Apr. 1977, 10-11; Sept. 1977, 21.

Bedford, Duke of, *Parrots and Parrotlike Birds*, Neptune City, NJ: T.F.H. Publications, Inc.

Buchan, James, "Housing Exotic Seedeaters," *American Cage Bird Magazine*, Dec. 1976, 28.

Buggie, Stephen, "Mexican Export Regulations on Birds," *American Cage Bird Magazine*, May 1977, 26.

Clear, Val, *Common Cagebirds in America*, Indianapolis, Indiana.: The Bobbs-Merrill Co. Inc., 1966. Division of birds into groups by singing ability, color, easily raised, hook-bills. Helpful in making choices and beginning to breed.

——, "Exotic Cage-Birds," *American Cage Bird Magazine*, Feb. 1980, 21.

——, *How to Make Money with Cage Birds*, Neptune City, NJ: T.F.H. Publications, 1980. Written for the person who wants to start on a small scale.

Fogg, Nola Miller, *Encyclopedia of Canaries and Other Cage Birds*, Chicago: Audubon Publishing Co., 1951. The basic book on Canaries.

Forshaw, Joseph M., *Parrots of the World*, Neptune City, NJ: T.F.H. Publications, Inc., 1977. Covers more Parrot species than Bates and Busenbark.

Gronholz, Bill, "Packing Birds for Shipping," *American Cage Bird Magazine*, Dec. 1974, 22.

Hall, Jo, *Cockatiels . . . Care and Breeding*, Austin, Tex.: Sweet Publishing Co., 1976.

Hart, Ernest H., *Budgerigar Handbook*, Neptune City, NJ: T.F.H. Publications, 1970.

Johns, Eric L., *What You Want to Know About Budgerigars*, London: Robert Hale and Co.; 1971. Beginning book on Budgies.

Joseph, Joan, *Pet Birds*, illus. John Hamberger, New York: Franklin, Watts Inc., 1975.

Kalvan, Jay and Hazel, "Housebreaking a Parrot!" *American Cage Bird Magazine*, Sept. 1975, 19.

Klingler, Kenneth, "Activities of Liberated Canaries," *American Cage Bird Magazine*, Jan. 1973, 12.

————, "Wintering in Outside Aviaries," *American Cage Bird Magazine*, Nov. 1977, 35.

Kranz, Frederick H. and Jacqueline L., *Gardening Indoors Under Lights*, New York: The Viking Press, revised edition, 1971.

Lindsay, William K., Ph.D., "Hospital Cages," *American Cage Bird Magazine*, March 1977, 21.

Martin, Alfred G., *Hand-Taming Wild Birds*, Freeport, Me.: The Bond Wheelwright Co., 1963.

Moon, Mrs. E.L., *Experiences with My Cockatiels*, Chicago: Audubon Publishing Co., 1976.

Olssen, Marie Earl, *Hookbills I Have Known*, Naples, Fla.: Private printing, 1977.

Reed, Nancy A., "Cinnamon and Pearlie Cockatiel Mutations," *American Cage Bird Magazine*, June 1977, 3.

————, "The Cockatiel," *The AFA Watchbird*, Oct./Nov. 1978, 6.

Roots, Clive, *Exotic Birds*, London: Casell, 1975.

————, "Feeding the Softbills," *American Cage Bird Magazine*, Oct. 1972, 7.

————, *Softbilled Birds*, New York: Arco Publishing Co., 1970. A must for those who own soft-bills.

Rogers, Cyril H., *Budgerigars*, revised edition, London: John Gifford, 1975.

————, *Encyclopedia of Cage and Aviary Birds*, New York: Macmillan Publishing Co., 1975. Reference on birds that are bred domestically; gives diet, housing, description of birds. Written in England; edited for the U.S. Birds are the same in both countries.

————, *Zebra Finches*, Leicester, England: K & R Books, Ltd., 1964.

Runnals, Mark, "Raising Your Own Seed," *American Cage Bird Magazine*, Oct. 1975, 6.

Smith, Jack, "There's a Swearing Bird on the Line," Cleveland *Plain Dealer*, June 14, 1977.

Tonge, Peter, "Chicken Raisers, Take Notice," *The Christian Science Monitor*, April 3, 1971.

Villiard, Paul, *Birds as Pets*, Garden City, N.Y.: Doubleday and Co. Inc., 1974.

Wahlin, William S., Ph.D., "Light . . . And the Breeding of Birds," *American Cage Bird Magazine*, Sept. 1977, 28.

INDEX

flying, 4, 19–22, 45, 86–87, 109. *See* wings, clipping of

fruit in diet, 52, 56–58, 61, 184–85

fruitflies in diet, 60

G

gizzard, function of, 45

glossary of terms, 192–96

Gouldian finches, 7, 55–56, 143–44

grass in diet, 54–55, 96

gravel, uses by birds, 44–46, 70, 127

gravel papers, 37

greens in diet. *See* vegetables and greens in diet

grooming: bill trimming, 74–75; claw trimming, 72–74. *See also* preening

H

hatching, 99

hawks, environmental role of, 136

head sitting, 87

holding birds, techniques for, 65–68, 86–87; finger-tamed birds, 4, 6, 18, 20, 66–67, 83, 87–88

honeycreepers, 59

hook-bills, 4, 19–22, 24, 29, 35, 45, 50, 74–75, 86–87, 89, 109; bird sitters for, 81–82; clipping wings of, 75; holding of, 66, 87; tricks by, 92–93

housebreaking of birds, 92

humidity, effects of, 42, 71–72, 115

I

import-export of birds, 6, 11, 107, 118–19, 121–23, 189. *See also* smuggling of birds

insect pests, 112–13

insects in diet, 48–49, 52, 58–62, 191. *See also* mealworms

International Bird Institute, 122

introducing birds to each other, 111

ABOUT THE AUTHOR

Neale Haley was born in Buffalo, New York, and is a graduate of Barnard College. Raising birds is a special hobby she shares with her husband. Their indoor aviary, she says, "gives us constant entertainment and a continuous education on bird habits. Baby birds from my aviary have been tamed by a score of children and young people, and many still have them as pets."

She lives in New Hampshire with her family.

ABOUT THE ILLUSTRATOR

Pamela Carroll has illustrated numerous books for children and adults, as well as newspaper and magazine articles. She lives in Westmoreland, New Hampshire.

BIRDS FOR PETS AND PLEASURE

Neale Haley

Illustrated by Pamela Carroll

Do you know which birds make the best pets? Why buying an imported bird may be dangerous? How to keep your bird happy and healthy?

These and scores of other questions about keeping birds for pets and pleasure are answered with affection and enthusiasm in this practical and reliable guide.

Beginning with how to choose the right bird for you, Neale Haley goes on to discuss housing, feeding, taming, and breeding birds. She also alerts readers to a serious threat to all birds today—smuggling. A comprehensive appendix provides complete instructions for building two kinds of aviaries and several outdoor feeders, as well as information on different species, breeders, and nutrition.

Illustrated with graceful, meticulous line drawings, this book is for anyone who cares about birds, whether in the house or free in the world.

NEALE HALEY was born in Buffalo, New York, and is a graduate of Barnard College. Raising birds is a special hobby she shares with her husband. Their indoor aviary, she says, "gives us constant entertainment and a continuous education on bird habits. Baby birds from my aviary have been tamed by a score of children and young people, and many still have them as pets."

Neale Haley lives in New Hampshire with her family.

PAMELA CARROLL has illustrated numerous books for children and adults, as well as newspaper and magazine articles. She lives in Westmoreland, New Hampshire.

"A pet bird is in a real sense another member of the family. We give it our affection and in return receive its unlimited love and trust. This book provides an important aid to making the pet bird genuinely a member of the family. Ms. Haley has written from years of experience with birds, and she has focused on practical *do's and don't's* that will answer questions and relieve the anxieties of bird lovers. The book deserves an honored place on a handy bookshelf; it will be consulted often as the bird leads its owner through the unfolding experiences of bird stewardship."

Val Clear
Contributing Editor
American Cage-Bird Magazine

DELACORTE PRESS/NEW YORK

$4.95

PRINTED IN U.S.A.

ISBN: 0-440-00475-6